WHO MA

THE CATECHIS

WHO MADE THE WORLD?

THE CATECHISM WE LEARNED IN SCHOOL

REV. DR JAMES BUTLER

MERCIER PRESS
5 French Church Street, Cork
and
16 Hume Street, Dublin 2

Trade enquiries to COLUMBA MERCIER DISTRIBUTION,
55a Spruce Avenue, Stillorgan Industrial Park, Blackrock, Dublin

© This edition, Mercier Press, 2001

ISBN: 1 85635 380 X

10 9 8 7 6 5 4 3 2 1

The publishers would like to thank Fr Christy O'Dwyer and Fr Patrick
Wallace for the background information on Archbishop James Butler
and his *Catechism*.

Printed in Ireland by Colour Books Ltd.

Publisher's Note

Whenever the topic of religious instruction in schools is raised today one is almost sure to hear members of an older generation express regret at the passing of the Butler Catechism. It occupies an unrivalled position among Irish catechisms and its influence extended far beyond Ireland. Those who learned the Butler Catechism in school need no reminding of its contents. Rarely will one meet former students of Catechism who cannot recite by heart awe-inspiring amounts of its profound and elegantly phrased answers. With determined and demanding teachers plus the prospect of a public examination before archbishop or bishop pupils had little option but to know their catechism!

Dr Butler, Archbishop of Cashel and Emly, wanted to ensure the proper instruction of young and old in Christian doctrine. The lack of a suitable textbook of Christian doctrine was felt at the time and his Catechism, composed in 1777, rectified this defect. The format of the Butler Catechism links it with a long chain of catechisms dating back two centuries to the Counter Reformation period when the general form and content of catechisms were determined by authors such as St Robert Bellarmine and St Peter Canisius. The Butler Catechism shares the strengths and weaknesses of this tradition. Anglo-Irish by birth and French by education, Dr Butler inevitably drew on sources that were outside the native Irish religious tradition. Consequently much of the earlier deeply spiritual Irish religious culture was not included in the Catechism and so was largely lost.

The first revision of the Butler Catechism in 1802 is testimony to the popularity of the original text. The initiative for the revised edition came from the state, which recognised Butler's text as the representative catechism for the country. A decade of social and political unrest, occasioned largely by the French Revolution, culminated in the bloodshed of the 1798 rebellion. The government approached the four archbishops with the suggestion that the duties of citizenship be further elaborated upon and strengthened in the Catechism. The 'revised, enlarged, approved and recommended ... General Catechism for the Kingdom' was the result. This catechism, known as the Butler General of 1802, was the product of this unusual alliance between the government and the four archbishops.

The National Synod of Bishops, which took place at Maynooth in 1875, initiated a project for a national catechism for the entire country. The result was a revision of the Butler General Catechism of 1802. For the first time, the name of Butler did not appear in the official title of the Catechism. But the 1882 revised edition was called the Maynooth-Butler Catechism.

The lifespan of National Catechism [1952] was short and the developments accompanying the Second Vatican Council ensured a rapid demise for the final heir to the Butler tradition of catechisms. Soon new texts, both native and imported, replaced the National Catechism – and Butler influence – in Irish schools. In its original edition and various revisions, it exerted a dominant influence on religious instruction in Ireland for almost two centuries.

That influence was to extend beyond Ireland, especially to the United States and Australia. The Butler Catechism travelled with Irish emigrants throughout the English-speaking world during the nineteenth century. It is not surprising that Irish clergy working with Irish exiles turned to the tried-and-tested Butler Catechism as a suitable text for the instruction of young exiles and their children. But the influence of the Catechism was not confined to the Irish alone. The compilers of the Baltimore Catechism (1884) in the United States made the Maynooth-Butler revision of 1882 one of their foundation texts. Almost half of the questions and answers in the Baltimore Catechism are found in the Butler Catechism. Canadian publishers printed the Butler Catechism in both the English and Irish languages. The Maynooth-Butler Catechism was adopted as the national catechism for Australia in 1885.

It is easy to be critical of weaknesses in Butler's Catechism, especially its limited theological understanding and its tendency to define and put everything in its place while perhaps overlooking the deeper mystery of the faith. Such criticisms are easy to make today, but given the purpose and context in which it was written the Butler Catechism was a remarkable document and its wide appeal and influence bear ample testimony to its excellence.

Dr James Butler II was a notable and respected figure in the Ireland of his day. His Catechism alone entitles him to a particular place in the history of the Irish Church over the last two centuries.

On 29 July 1791 Dr Butler, Archbishop of Cashel and Emly, died. He was forty-nine years of age and his remains now lie under the sanctuary of Thurles Cathedral.

PRAYER TABLET

In the Name of the Father, and of the Son, and of the Holy Ghost. *Amen.*

The Lord's Prayer
Our Father, who art in Heaven, hallowed be Thy name; Thy kingdom come; Thy will be done on earth as it is in Heaven. Give us this day our daily bread, and forgive us our trespasses as we forgive them who trespass against us; and lead us not into temptation, but deliver us from evil. *Amen.*

The Angelical Salutation
Hail Mary, full of grace, the Lord is with thee; blessed art thou among women, and blessed is the fruit of thy womb, Jesus. Holy Mary, Mother of God, pray for us sinners, now, and at the hour of our death. *Amen.*

Glory be to the Father
Glory be to the Father, and to the Son, and to the Holy Ghost, as it was in the beginning, is now and ever shall be, world without end. *Amen.*

The Apostles' Creed
I believe in God, the Father Almighty, Creator of Heaven and earth, and in Jesus Christ, His only Son, our Lord, who was conceived of the Holy Ghost, born of the Virgin Mary; suffered under Pontius Pilate; was crucified, died, and was buried; He descended into Hell; the third day He rose again from the dead; He ascended into Heaven, and sitteth at the

right hand of God, the Father Almighty, from thence He shall come to judge the living and the dead. I believe in the Holy Ghost, the Holy Catholic Church, the communion of saints, the forgiveness of sins, the resurrection of the body, and life everlasting. *Amen*.

Morning Offering

O my God, I adore Thee, I love Thee, I offer Thee my heart, my soul, my body, with all my thoughts, words, actions, pains and sufferings, that they may be all to Thy glory and my salvation, through Christ our Lord. *Amen*.

The Confiteor

I confess to Almighty God, to the blessed Mary ever Virgin, to blessed Michael the Archangel, to blessed John the Baptist, to the holy Apostles Peter and Paul, and to all the saints, that I have sinned exceedingly in thought, word, and deed, through my fault, through my fault, through my most grievous fault. Therefore I beseech the blessed Mary ever Virgin, blessed Michael the Archangel, blessed John the Baptist, the holy Apostles Peter and Paul, and all the saints, to pray to the Lord our God for me. *Amen*.

May the Almighty God have mercy on me, forgive me my sins, and bring me to life everlasting. *Amen*.

May the Almighty and merciful Lord grant me pardon, absolution, and remission of all my sins. *Amen*.

Act of Contrition
O my God, I am sorry for my sins because Thou art so good, and with Thy help I will never sin again.

Act of Faith
O my God, I believe in Thee and in all Thy Holy Church teaches, because Thou hast said it, and Thy word is true.

Act of Hope
O my God, I hope in Thee for grace and glory, because of Thy promises, Thy mercy, and Thy power.

Act of Charity
O my God, because Thou art infinitely good and perfect, I love Thee with my whole heart, and for Thy sake I love my neighbour as myself. (*7 years and 7 quarantines each time.*)

Prayer to Guardian Angel
O Angel of God, to whose holy care I am committed by the Supreme clemency, illuminate, defend, and keep me this day from all sin and danger. *Amen.*

Night Offering
Jesus, Mary, and Joseph, I give you my heart and my soul.
Jesus, Mary, and Joseph, assist me in my last agony.
Jesus, Mary, and Joseph, may I breathe forth my soul in peace with you.
Into Thy hands, O God, I commend my spirit.
Lord Jesus, receive my soul.

Prayer before the Acts

O Almighty and Eternal God, grant unto us an increase of faith, hope, and charity; and that we may obtain what Thou hast promised, make us to love and practise what Thou commandest: through Jesus Christ our Lord. *Amen*.

Act of Contrition

O my God, I am heartily sorry for having offended Thee, and I detest my sins most sincerely, because they displease Thee, my God, who, for Thy Infinite goodness and most amiable perfections, art so deserving of all my love; and I firmly purpose, by Thy holy grace, never more to offend Thee, and to amend my life.

Act of Faith

O my God, I firmly believe that Thou art one only God, the Creator and Sovereign Lord of Heaven and earth, infinitely great and infinitely good. I firmly believe that in Thee, one only God, there are three Divine Persons, really distinct, and equal in all things – the Father, and the Son, and the Holy Ghost. I firmly believe that God the Son, the second person of the Most Holy Trinity, became man, that He was conceived of the Holy Ghost, and was born of the Virgin Mary, that He suffered and died on a cross to redeem and save us; that He rose the third day from the dead; that He ascended into Heaven; that He will come at the end of the world to judge mankind; that He will reward the good with eternal happiness, and condemn the wicked to the everlasting pains of Hell. I believe these and all other articles which the Holy

Catholic Church proposes to our belief, because Thou, my God, the Infallible Truth, hast revealed them; and Thou has commanded us to hear the Church, which is the pillar and the ground of truth. In this faith I am firmly resolved, by Thy holy grace, to live and die. *(Matt. xviii. 17; Tim. iii. 15)*

Act of Hope

O my God, who has graciously promised every blessing, even Heaven itself, through Jesus Christ, to those who keep Thy commandments; relying on Thy infinite power, goodness, and mercy, and on Thy sacred promises to which Thou art always faithful, I confidently hope to obtain pardon of all my sins, grace to serve Thee faithfully in this life, by doing the good works Thou has commanded, which, with Thy assistance, I now purpose to perform, and eternal happiness in the next, through my Lord and Saviour Jesus Christ.

Act of Charity

O my God, I love Thee with my whole heart and soul, and above all things, because Thou art infinitely good and perfect, and most worthy of all my love; and for Thy sake I love my neighbour as myself. Mercifully grant, O my God, that having loved Thee on earth, I may love and enjoy Thee forever in Heaven. *Amen.*

The Angelus Domini

1. The Angel of the Lord declared unto Mary:
And she conceived of the Holy Ghost.

Hail Mary, full of grace, the Lord is with thee; blessed art thou among women, and blessed is the fruit of thy womb,

Jesus. Holy Mary, Mother of God, pray for us sinners, now, and at the hour of our death. *Amen.*

2. Behold the handmaid of the Lord:
Be it done unto me according to Thy word.
Hail Mary ... Holy Mary ...

3. And the Word was made flesh:
And dwelt amongst us.
Hail Mary ... Holy Mary ...

Pray for us, O holy Mother of God.
That we may be made worthy of the promises of Christ.

LET US PRAY
Pour forth, we beseech Thee, O Lord, Thy grace into our hearts, that we, to whom the incarnation of Christ, Thy Son, was made known by the message of an angel, may by His passion and cross be brought to the glory of His resurrection, through the same Christ our Lord. *Amen.*

May the Divine assistance always remain with us.

And may the souls of the faithful departed through the mercy of God, rest in peace *Amen.*

Memorare

Remember, O most tender Virgin Mary, that it was never known that anyone who fled to thy protection, implored thy help, or sought thy intercession was left unaided. Inspired with this confidence, I fly unto thee, O Virgin of Virgins, my Mother; to thee I come, before thee I stand, sinful and sorrowful; O Mother of the word Incarnate, despise not my petitions, but in thy clemency hear and answer me. *Amen*. (*300 days each time. Plenary once a month*)

Prayer to St Joseph

We beseech Thee, O Lord, to help us through the merits of the spouse of Thy most holy Mother; and what our own efforts cannot obtain, do Thou grant us through his intercession; who livest and reignest world without end. *Amen*.

Prayer to the Sacred Heart

To Thee, O Sacred Heart of Jesus, I offer and consecrate my heart and my whole being for time and eternity. O heart the most tender, the most gentle, the most kind, be Thou the sole object of my love, the protector of my life, and my secure refuge at the hour of death. *Amen*.

Grace before Meals

Bless us, O Lord, and these Thy gifts which of Thy bounty we are about to receive, through Christ our Lord. *Amen*.

Grace after Meals

We give Thee thanks, O Almighty God, for all Thy benefits, who livest and reignest, world without end. *Amen*.

May the souls of the faithful departed, through Mercy of God, rest in peace. *Amen.*

The Divine Praises

Blessed be God.

Blessed be His Holy Name.

Blessed be Jesus Christ, true God and true man.

Blessed be the Name of Jesus.

Blessed be His Most Sacred Heart.

Blessed be Jesus in the Most Holy Sacrament of the Altar.

Blessed be the great Mother of God, Mary most holy

Blessed be her holy and Immaculate Conception.

Blessed be the name of Mary, Virgin and Mother.

Blessed be God in His Angels and in His Saints.

(2 years each time)

Prayer to St Patrick

O God, who didst send amongst us Thy blessed servant, St Patrick, and didst inspire him with such love and zeal for the Irish nation, grant us by his powerful intercession ever to love and honour that holy faith which he planted in our midst, and so to regulate our lives that we may one day reign with him in the kingdom of Thy glory. *Amen.*

THE MYSTERIES OF THE ROSARY

The Joyful Mysteries

1. The Annunciation
2. The Visit to St Elizabeth
3. The Birth of our Lord
4. The Presentation of our Lord in the Temple
5. The Finding of our Lord in the Temple

The Sorrowful Mysteries

1. The Agony in the Garden
2. The Scourging at the Pillar
3. The Crowning with Thorns
4. The Carrying of the Cross
5. The Crucifixion

The Glorious Mysteries

1. The Resurrection
2. The Ascension
3. The Descent of the Holy Ghost
4. The Assumption of the Blessed Virgin
5. The Crowning of the Blessed Virgin

Indulgenced Ejaculatory Prayers

Sweet Heart of Jesus, be Thou my love. (*300 days each time*)

Immaculate Heart of Mary, pray for us. (*100 days each time*)

Dear St Joseph, our guide, protect us and the Holy Church.
(*50 days each time*)

Jesus, Mary. (*25 days each time*)

O Sacred Heart of Jesus, I implore that I may love Thee daily
more and more. (*300 days each time*)

Jesus, meek and humble of heart, make my heart like unto
Thine. (*300 days each time*)

My Jesus, mercy; Mary, help. (*100 days each time*)

Sweet Jesus, be not to me a judge, but a Saviour. (*50 days each
time*)

Eternal Father, I offer Thee the Precious Blood of Jesus in
satisfaction for my sins, and for the wants of Holy Church.
(*100 days each time*)

May the Sacred Heart of Jesus be everywhere loved. (*100 days each time*)

May the most just, the most high, and the most, adorable will of God, be in all things done, praised and magnified forever. (*100 days each time*)

Blessed and praised every moment be the most holy and Divine Sacrament. (*100 days. Plenary once a month*)

Prayers after Low Mass

Hail Mary, &c., three times.

Hail, holy Queen, Mother of Mercy, hail, our life, our sweetness, and our hope. To thee do we cry, poor banished children of Eve. To thee do we send up our sighs, mourning and weeping in this valley of tears. Turn, then, most gracious advocate, thine eyes of mercy towards us; and after this our exile, show unto us the blessed fruit of thy womb, Jesus. O clement, O loving, O sweet Virgin Mary.

V. Pray for us, O holy Mother of God.

R. That we may be made worthy of the promises of Christ.

LET US PRAY

O God, our refuge and our strength, look down with favour on Thy people who cry to Thee; and through the intercession of the glorious and Immaculate Virgin Mother of God, of St Joseph her spouse, of Thy blessed Apostles Peter and Paul, and of all the saints, in mercy and goodness hear our prayers for the conversion of sinners, and for the liberty and exaltation of our holy mother the Church, through the same Christ our Lord. *Amen.*

Blessed Michael, Archangel, defend us in the hour of conflict; be our safeguard against the wickedness and snares of the devil – may God restrain him, we humbly pray: and do thou, O Prince of the Heavenly host, by the power of God, thrust Satan down to Hell, and, with him the other wicked spirits who wander through the world for the ruin of souls. *Amen*. (*300 days each time*)

Most Sacred Heart of Jesus, have mercy on us.
Most Sacred Heart of Jesus, have mercy on us.
Most Sacred Heart of Jesus, have mercy on us. (*7 years and 7 quarantines*)

The Stations of the Cross

1   Jesus is condemned to Death
2   Jesus is laden with the Cross
3   Jesus falls the First Time
4   Jesus meets His Blessed Mother
5   Simon of Cyrene helps Jesus to carry the Cross
6   Jesus meets Veronica
7   Jesus falls a Second Time
8   Jesus comforts the women of Jerusalem
9   Jesus falls a Third Time
10 Jesus is stripped of His garments
11 Jesus is nailed to the Cross
12 Jesus dies on the Cross
13 Jesus is taken down from the Cross
14 Jesus is laid in the Sepulchre

En Ego

Look down, O good and gentle Jesus, on me humbly pros-
trate before Thee: with the most fervent desire of my soul I
pray and beseech Thee that Thou wouldst impress upon my
heart lively sentiments of faith, hope, and charity, true contrition for my sins, and a firm purpose of amendment; while
with deep affliction and grief of soul I ponder within myself
and mentally contemplate Thy five most Precious Wounds;
having before my eyes the words which David, the Prophet,
put into Thy mouth concerning Thee, O good Jesus: *They
have dug My hands and feet; they have numbered all My bones.*

(A plenary indulgence may be gained by those who, after Confession
and Communion, recite this prayer before a representation of Christ
crucified and pray for the intention of the Sovereign Pontiff.)

Anima Christi

Soul of Christ, sanctify me.
Body of Christ, save me.
Blood of Christ, inebriate me.
Water from the side of Christ, cleanse me.
Passion of Christ, strengthen me.
O good Jesus, graciously hear me.
Within Thy wounds hide me.
Suffer me not to be separated from Thee.
From the malignant enemy defend me.
At the hour of my death call me,
And bid me come to Thee,
That, with Thy Saints, I may praise Thee
For all eternity. *Amen.*

(*300 days each time; 7 years, after Communion*)

THE CATECHISM

LESSON I

ON GOD AND THE CREATION OF THE WORLD

World	*the whole creation*
Creator	*one who makes out of nothing*
Sovereign	*supreme*
Lord	*master*
Reward	*to repay*
Principally	*chiefly*
Manifests	*shows*
Kingdom	*possessions of a king*
Saint	*one who dies in the state of grace, and whose soul is now in Heaven*
Spirit	*a being who cannot be seen or felt*
Corporal	*belonging to the body*
Continually	*always*
Secret	*hidden*
Idle word	*a useless word*
Render	*to give*
Possible	*capable of being done*
Difficult	*hard*

Q. Who made the world?

A. God made the world.

Q. Who is God?

A. The Creator and Sovereign Lord of Heaven and earth, and of all things.

Q. How many Gods are there?

A. There is but one God, who will reward the good, and punish the wicked.

Q. Where is God?

A. God is everywhere, but is said principally to be in Heaven, where He manifests Himself to the blessed.

Q. What is Heaven?

A. The kingdom of God's glory, and of His angels and saints.

Q. If God be everywhere, why do we not see Him?

A. Because God is a pure spirit, having no body, and therefore cannot be seen with corporal eyes.

Q. Does God see us?

A. He does, and continually watches over us.

Q. Does God know all things?

A. Yes; all things are naked and open to His eyes, even our most secret thoughts and actions. (*Heb. iv. 13*)

Q. Will God judge our most secret thoughts and actions?

A. Yes; and every idle word that men shall speak they shall render an account for it on the day of judgement. (*Matt. xii. 36*)

Q. Had God a beginning?

A. No; He always was, and always will be.

Q. Can God do all things?

A. Yes; with God all things are possible, and nothing can be difficult to Him. (*Matt. xix. 26*)

Q. How did God make the world?

A. Of nothing; and by His word only – that is, by a single act of His all-powerful will.

Q. Why did God make the world?

A. For His own glory, to show His power and wisdom, and for man's use and benefit. (*Psalms xviii*)

ON MAN AND THE END OF HIS CREATION

Creature	*anything created*
Composed	*made up of*
Soul	*immortal part of man*
Immortal	*not subject to death*
Capable	*having power*
Fulfil	*to accomplish*
Truths	*things that are true*
Apostle	*one sent*

Q. What is man?

A. One of God's creatures composed of a body and soul, and made to God's likeness.

Q. In what is man made to God's likeness?

A. In his soul.

Q. In what is man's soul like to God?

A. In being a spirit, and immortal, and in being capable of knowing and loving God.

21

Q. What do you mean when you say that the soul is immortal?

A. I mean that it can never die.

Q. Why did God give us souls capable of knowing and loving Him?

A. That we might fulfil the end for which He made us.

Q. For what end did God make us?

A. To know and serve Him here on earth, and after to see and enjoy Him forever in Heaven.

Q. How can we know God on earth?

A. By learning the truths He has taught.

Q. Where shall we find the truths God has taught?

A. They are chiefly contained in the Apostles' Creed.

LESSON III

ON THE APOSTLES' CREED

Creed	*what a person believes, a short rule of faith*
Mysteries	*truths that cannot be understood*
Religion	*the science which teaches us to know and serve God*
Articles	*truths to be believed*
Unity	*one*
Trinity	*three in one*
Unerring	*true*
Incarnation	*taking flesh*
Resurrection	*rising from the dead*
Explicitly	*directly, and with a clear distinct knowledge. Explicit belief is a belief accompanied by a definite, distinct knowledge of the particular truth in which a person believes*

Grounded	*built upon*
Revealed	*made known*
Comprehend	*to understand*
Homage	*worship*
Submit	*to yield*
Incomprehensible	*not to be understood*
Supreme	*highest*

Q. What does the Apostles' Creed contain?

A. The principal mysteries of religion and other necessary articles.

Q. Which are the principal mysteries of religion?

A. The Unity and Trinity of God, the Incarnation, Death, and Resurrection of our Saviour.

Q. Why are they called principal mysteries?

A. Because these five mysteries are most necessary to be explicitly believed, and because all other mysteries of religion are grounded on them. *(John xvii. 3)*

Q. What do you mean by mysteries of religion?

A. Revealed truths which we cannot comprehend.

Q. Does God require of us to believe mysteries of religion?

A. Yes; God requires of us to pay Him the homage of our understanding, and to submit our will to Him in all things.

Q. How do we pay the homage of our understanding to God?

A. By firmly believing on God's unerring word whatever He has revealed, be it ever so incomprehensible to us.

23

Q. How do we submit our will to God?

A. By cheerfully doing, in obedience to God, all things whatsoever He commands.

Q. What means the unity of God?

A. It means that there is but one God, and that there cannot be more Gods than one. (*Eph. iv. 6*)

Q. Why cannot there be more Gods than one?

A. Because God, being a supreme and sovereign Lord, cannot have an equal.

LESSON IV

ON THE TRINITY AND THE INCARNATION

Divine	*relating to God*
Distinct	*separate*
Eternity	*without beginning or end*
Perfections	*qualities that make us perfect; all God's qualities are perfections*
Assumed	*took*
Human	*relating to man*
Operation	*work*
Anointed	*rubbed with oil*
Redeem	*to release; to buy back*
Passion	*sufferings*
Forbidden	*hindered*

Q. How many persons are there in God?

A. Three divine Persons, really distinct, and equal in all things. (*I. John, v. 7*)

Q. How do you call the three divine Persons?

A. The Father, the Son, and the Holy Ghost.

Q. Is the Father God?

A. Yes; the Father is God, and the first Person of the Blessed Trinity.

Q. Is the Son God?

A. Yes; the Son is God, and the second Person of the Blessed Trinity.

Q. Is the Holy Ghost God?

A. Yes; the Holy Ghost is God, and the third Person of the Blessed Trinity.

Q. What means the Blessed Trinity?

A. One God in three divine Persons.

Q. Are the three divine Persons three Gods?

A. No; they are only one God, having but one and the same divine nature; and they are from eternity.

Q. Is any of the three divine Persons more powerful or more wise than the others?

A. No; as the three divine Persons are all but one and the same God, they must be alike in all divine perfections; therefore one cannot be more powerful or more wise than the others.

Q. Did one of the three divine Persons become man?

A. Yes; God the Son, the second Divine person became man.
    (John i. 14)

Q. How did God the Son become man?

A. He was conceived of the Holy Ghost and born of the Virgin Mary. *(Ap. Cr.)*

Q. What do you mean by saying that the Son of God was conceived of the Holy Ghost?

A. I mean that He assumed human nature, that is, a body and soul like ours, by the power and operation of the Holy Ghost.

Q. Where did God the Son take a body and soul like ours?

A. In the chaste womb of the Virgin Mary, and He was born man of her.

Q. How do you call God the Son made man?

A. Jesus Christ.

Q. What is the meaning of these words, Jesus Christ?

A. Jesus signifies Saviour, and Christ signifies the anointed; and St Paul says that, *at the name of Jesus every knee should bend.* (*Phil. ii. 10*)

Q. Did. Jesus Christ remain God when He became man?

A. Yes; He was always God.

Q. Was Jesus Christ always man?

A. No; only from the time of His conception or incarnation.

Q. What means the incarnation?

A. That God the Son, the second Person of the Blessed Trinity, was made man.

Q. What do you believe Jesus Christ to be?

A. True God and true man.

Q. Why did Christ become man?

A. To redeem and save us.

Q. How did Christ redeem and save us?

A. By His sufferings and death on the cross.

Q. Was it by His passion and death also Christ satisfied the justice of God for our sins?

A. Yes; and by these He delivered us from Hell and from the power of the devil.

ON OUR FIRST PARENTS

Sensible	*perceiving with the mind or the senses; convinced, or having a feeling of the existence of anything*
Obedience	*submission to lawful authority*
Envying	*grudging, feeling pained by another's happiness*
Dependence	*requiring support*
Dominion	*authority*
Tempted	*enticed to evil*
Rebellious	*opposed to lawful authority*
Adore	*to give supreme honour*
Enjoy	*to possess*
Minister	*to attend to*
Guardians	*protectors*
Torments	*punishments*
Mortal	*deadly*
Confirmed	*established*

Q. How came we into the power of the devil?

A. By the disobedience of our first parents in eating the forbidden fruit. (*Gen. ii. iii*)

Q. Who were our first parents?

A. Adam and Eve, the first man and woman.

Q. Why did God command our first parents not to eat the forbidden fruit?

A. To make them sensible of His dominion over them, and of their dependence on Him and to try their obedience.

Q. Who tempted our first parents to eat the forbidden fruit?

A. The devil, envying their happy state. (*Gen. iii*)

Q. Whom do you mean by the devil?

A. One of the rebellious or fallen angels whom God cast out of Heaven.

Q. What do you mean by angels?

A. Pure spirits without a body, created to adore and enjoy God in Heaven.

Q. Were the angels created for any other purpose?

A. Yes; to assist before the throne of God, and to minister unto Him; and they have been often sent as messengers from God to man, and are also appointed our guardians. (*Apoc. vii. 9, 11; Heb. i. 7; Matt. iv. 6, xviii. 10*)

Q. Why were any angels cast out of Heaven?

A. Because through pride, they rebelled against God. (*Isaias xiv*)

Q. Did God punish in any other way the angels who rebelled?

A. Yes; He condemned them to Hell, a place of eternal torments.

Q. Why did God make Hell?

A. To punish the devils or bad angels.

Q. Are any others condemned to Hell besides the devils or bad angels?

A. Yes; all who die enemies to God, that is, all who die in the state of mortal sin.

Q. Can anyone come out of Hell?

A. No, out of Hell there is no redemption.

Q. How did God reward the angels who remained faithful?

A. He confirmed them forever in glory.

LESSON VI
ON ORIGINAL SIN, &c

Paradise	*the garden of Eden*
Original	*first*
Posterity	*descendants*
Deprived	*took from*
Partakers	*sharers*
Inherit	*to receive by descent*
Wrath	*anger*
Transmitted	*passed from one to another*
Infected	*diseased*
Immaculate	*without stain*
Origin	*beginning*
Effects	*consequences*
Corrupted	*infected*
Will	*inclination*
Inclination	*a tendency*
Temporal	*relating to time*
Occasion	*cause*
Resisting	*fighting against*
Original justice	*the grace given by God to our first parents when they were created*
Innocence	*freedom from guilt*
Conception	*the act of being conceived*

Q. How did God punish the disobedience of our first parents?

A. They were driven out of Paradise, stripped of original justice and innocence, and condemned to death with all their posterity.

Q. Did God inflict any other punishment on our first parents?

A. Yes; He deprived them of all right to Heaven, and of several other blessings intended for them.

Q. What were the chief blessings intended for our first parents?

A. A constant state of happiness if they remained faithful to God.

Q. Were we condemned to the same punishments with our first parents?

A. Yes; we were all made partakers of their sin and punishments, as we would be all sharers in their innocence and happiness if they had been obedient to God. (*Rom. v. 12*)

Q. How do you call the sin of our first parents?

A. Original sin.

Q. What is original sin?

A. The sin we inherit from our first parents, and in which we are conceived and born children of wrath. (*Eph. ii. 3*)

Q. Why is it called original sin?

A. Because it is transmitted to us from our first parents, and we came into the world infected with it; and because it is the origin and source of every evil and misery to us. (*Rom. v. 12*)

Q. What other particular effects follow from the sin of our first parents?

A. Our whole nature was corrupted by it, it darkened our understanding, weakened our will, and left in us a strong inclination to evil.

Q. What is the reason that this darkness of the understanding, this weakness of the will, and this propensity to evil still remain, together with many other temporal punishments, even after original sin is forgiven?

A. To serve as an occasion of merit to us; by resisting our corrupt inclinations, and by bearing patiently the sufferings of this life.

Q. Have all the descendants of our first parents inherited original sin?

A. All have, except the Blessed Virgin Mary, the Mother of our Lord Jesus Christ.

Q. How was she preserved from it?

A. By a singular grace bestowed on her by God through the merits of her Divine Son.

Q. What is this singular privilege of the Blessed Virgin called?

A. It is called her Immaculate Conception.

Transgression	*a fault*
Annunciation	*making known*
Announced	*made known*
Crucified	*nailed to a cross*
Ignominious	*shameful*
Excess	*more than enough*
Jews	*followers of the Old Law*
Infer	*to learn*
Enormity	*grievousness*
Satisfying	*paying*

Q. Did God the Son become man immediately after the transgression of our first parents?

A. No; though He was immediately promised to them as a Redeemer. (*Gen. iii. 15*)

Q. How many years after the fall of our first parents did God the Son become man?

A. About four thousand years.

Q. How could they be saved who lived before God the Son became man?

A. By the belief of a Redeemer to come, and by keeping the commandments of God.

Q. On what day did God the Son become man?

A. On the twenty-fifth of March, the day of the annunciation; He was conceived of the Holy Ghost. (*Ap. Cr.*)

Q. Why is it called the day of the annunciation?

A. Because on that day the Angel Gabriel announced to the Virgin Mary: *Behold thou shalt conceive in thy womb, and shalt bring forth a son, and thou shalt call his name Jesus.* (*Luke i. 31*)

Q. On what day was Christ born of the Virgin Mary?

A. On Christmas Day, in a stable at Bethlehem.

Q. How long did Christ live on earth?

A. About thirty-three years, He led a most holy life in poverty and sufferings.

Q. Why did Christ live so long on earth?

A. To show us the way to Heaven by His instructions and example.

Q. How did Christ end His life?

A. On Good Friday He was crucified on Mount Calvary, and died nailed to a cross. (*Ap. Cr.*)

Q. Why do you call that day good, on which Christ suffered so painful and ignominious a death?

A. Because on that day, by dying on the cross, He showed the excess of His love, and purchased every blessing for us.

Q. Who condemned Christ to so cruel a death?

A. Pontius Pilate, the Roman Governor, did it at the desire of the Jews.

Q. What do you infer from the sufferings and death of Christ?

A. The enormity of sin, the hatred God bears to it, and the necessity of satisfying for it.

Q. Did anything remarkable happen at the death of Christ?

A. Yes; the sun darkened, the earth trembled, and the dead arose and appeared to many. (*Matt. xxvii*)

LESSON VIII

ON CHRIST'S DESCENT INTO HELL, AND ON HIS RESURRECTION
AND ASCENSION INTO HEAVEN

Descent	*to go down*
Tidings	*news*
Redemption	*release; buying back*
Ascend	*to go up*
Abide	*to live with*

Q. Where did Christ's soul go after His death?

A. It descended into Hell. (*Ap. Cr.*)

Q. Did Christ's soul descend into the Hell of the damned?

A. No; but to a place or state of rest called limbo. (*Acts ii. 24, 27; Ps. xv. 10*)

35

Q. Who were in limbo?

A. The souls of the saints who died before Christ.

Q. Why did Christ descend into limbo?

A. St Peter says to preach to those spirits who were in prison; that is, to announce to them in person the joyful tidings of their redemption. (*Peter iii. 19*)

Q. Why did not the souls of the saints who died before Christ go to Heaven immediately after their death?

A. Because Heaven was shut against them by the sin of our first parents, and could not be opened to anyone but by the death of Christ.

Q. When did the souls of the saints who died before Christ go to Heaven?

A. When Christ ascended into Heaven.

Q. Where was Christ's body while His soul was in limbo?

A. In the sepulchre or grave.

Q. On what day did Christ rise from the dead?

A. On Easter Sunday, the third day after He was crucified, He arose in body and soul, glorious and immortal from the dead. (*Ap. Cr.*)

Q. What does the resurrection of Christ prove?

A. It proves in the clearest possible way that He was God, for if He were not God He could not raise Himself from the dead.

Q. What does His death prove?

A. Among many other things, it proves that He was a real mortal man. He could not die unless He had another nature besides the divine nature.

Q. How long did Christ stay on earth after His resurrection?

A. Forty days; to show that He was truly risen from the dead, and to instruct His apostles.

Q. After Christ had remained forty days on earth, where did He go?

A. On Ascension Day He ascended from Mount Olivet, with His body and soul into Heaven. (*Ap. Cr.*)

Q. Where is Christ in Heaven?

A. He sits at the right hand of God the Father Almighty. (*Ap. Cr.*)

Q. What do you mean by saying that Christ sits at the right hand of God?

A. I mean that Christ, as God, is equal to His Father in all things; and, as man, is in the highest place in Heaven, next to God in power and glory.

Q. What did Christ promise to His apostles before He ascended into Heaven?

A. That He would send the Holy Ghost, the Spirit of truth, to teach them all things, and to abide with them forever. (*John xiv. 16, 17*)

On the Descent of the Holy Ghost, on the New Law, and on the Sign of the Cross

Tongues	*languages*
Scripture	*the written word of God*
Divers	*several*
Sanctify	*to make holy*
Gospel	*good news*
Established	*founded*
Christians	*followers of Christ*
Profess	*to declare openly*
Doctrine	*teaching*
Frequently	*very often*
Temptation	*an enticement to evil*
Invoke	*to call upon*
Church	*a congregation*

Q. On what day, and after what manner, did the Holy Ghost descend on the apostles?

A. On Whit-Sunday, the Holy Ghost descended in the form of tongues of fire, and sat upon everyone of them. *(Acts ii)*

Q. What does the Scripture say of those who received the Holy Ghost?

A. *They are all filled with the Holy Ghost, and they began to speak in divers tongues the wonderful works of God. (Acts ii)*

Q. Why did Christ send the Holy Ghost?

A. To sanctify His Church, to comfort His apostles, and to enable them to preach the gospel, or the new law.

Q. What do you mean by the new law?

A. The law which Christ established on earth.

Q. Which was the old law?

A. The law given to the Jews.

Q. How do you call the followers of the new law?

A. Christians.

Q. How are we known to be Christians?

A. By being baptised, by professing the doctrine of Christ, and by the sign of the cross.

Q. How is the sign of the cross made?

A. By putting the right hand to the forehead, then under the breast, then to the left and right shoulders, saying: *In the name of the Father, and of the Son, and of the Holy Ghost. Amen.*

Q. Why do we make the sign of the cross?

A. To beg that Jesus Christ, by His cross and passion, may bless and protect us.

Q. Should we frequently make the sign of the cross?

A. Yes, particularly in all temptations and dangers, and before and after prayer but always with great attention and devotion.

Q. What does the sign of the cross signify?

A. It signifies and brings to our minds the principal mysteries of religion.

Q. What mysteries of religion does the sign of the cross recall to our minds?

A. The Blessed Trinity, and the Incarnation and Death of our Saviour.

Q. How does the sign of the cross remind us of the Blessed Trinity?

A. Because in making the sign of the cross, we invoke the three divine Persons, saying: *In the name of the Father, and of the Son, and of the Holy Ghost.*

Q. How does the sign of the cross bring to our mind the incarnation and death of our Saviour?

A. Because, as He suffered death in human flesh on a cross, the sign of the cross must naturally remind all true Christians of His incarnation and death.

Q. Where are true Christians to be found?

A. Only in the True Church.

Lesson X
On the True Church

Pastors	the clergy
Visible	able to be seen
Catholic	universal
Moral	just; in keeping with the moral law
Salvation	saving, entrance into Heaven
Enlivened	made active
Faith	belief
Charity	love
Impossible	not able to be done
Justified	made just
Distribute	to give out
Apostolical	belonging to the Apostles
Fold	a place for a flock, or the flock
Animated	enlivened
Members	those who make up a body
Sacrifice	an offering made to God
Eminent	remarkable
Subsisted	existed
Successor	one who follows in the place of another

Q. What do you mean by the True Church?

A. The congregation of all the faithful, who, being baptised, profess the same doctrine, partake of the same sacraments, and are governed by their lawful pastors under one visible head on earth.

Q. How do you call the True Church?

A. The Holy Catholic Church. (*Ap. Cr.*)

Q. Is there any other True Church besides the Holy Catholic Church?

A. No; as there is but one Lord, one Faith, one Baptism, one God, and Father of all, there is but one True Church. (*Ephes. iv. 5, 6*)

41

Q. Are all obliged to be of the True Church?

A. Yes; no one can be saved out of it. (*Acts ii; John x; Matt. xxviii*)

Q. Will strict honesty to everyone, and moral good works, insure salvation, whatever Church or religion one professes?

A. No; unless such good works be enlivened by faith that worketh by charity. (*Gal. v. 6*)

Q. Why must our good works be enlivened by faith?

A. Because the Scripture says, *without faith it is impossible to please God; and he that believeth not shall be condemned.* (*Heb. xi. 6; Mark xvi. 16*)

Q. Are we justified by faith alone without good works?

A. No; as the body without the spirit is dead, so also faith without good works is dead. (*Jas. ii. 26*)

Q. Must our good works be also enlivened by charity?

A. Yes; for St Paul says, *if I should distribute all my goods to feed the poor, and if I should deliver my body to be burned, and have not charity, it profiteth me nothing.* (*I. Cor. xiii. 3*)

Q. What is that charity of which St Paul speaks?

A. That pure and sincere love of God, which makes us do His will in all things, and to be obedient to His Church, which He commands us to hear. (*Matt. xviii. 17; Luke x. 16*)

Q. Which are the marks or signs of the True Church?

A. The True Church is One, Holy, Catholic, and Apostolical.

Q. How is the Church one?

A. In being one body and one fold, animated by one spirit, under one head, and one shepherd, Jesus Christ, who is over all the Church. (*Eph. i. iv*)

Q. In what else is the Church one?

A. In all its members believing the same truths, having the same sacraments and sacrifice, and being under one visible head on earth.

Q. How is the Church holy?

A. In its founder, Jesus Christ; in its doctrine and sacraments; and in the number of its children, who have been eminent for holiness in all ages.

Q. How is the Church catholic or universal?

A. Because it has subsisted in every age, and is to last to the end of time, and will be spread throughout all nations. (*Matt. xxviii; Rom. x*)

Q. How is the Church apostolical?

A. Because it was founded by Christ on His apostles, and was governed by them, and, since the time of the apostles, it has always been governed by their lawful successors; and because it never ceased, and never will cease to teach their doctrine. (*Ephes. ii. 20*)

Peter	*rock*
See	*the residence of a bishop*
Pope	*father*
Vicar	*substitute; one who acts for another*
Text	*a sentence from Scripture*
Committed	*gave in charge*
Scripture	*the written word of God*
Err	*to go wrong*
Consummation	*the end*
Prevail	*to have power*
Communion	*union amongst many*

Q. Why do you call the Church 'Roman'?

A. Because the visible head of the Church is Bishop of Rome; and because St Peter and his successors fixed their see at Rome.

Q. Who is the visible head of the Church?

A. The Pope, who is Christ's Vicar on earth, and supreme visible head of the Church.

Q. To whom does the Pope succeed as visible head of the Church?

A. To St Peter, who was chief of the apostles, Christ's Vicar on earth, and first Pope and Bishop of Rome.

Q. When was St Peter made Pope or head of the Church?

A. Chiefly when Christ said to him, *thou art Peter, and upon this rock I will build my Church, and I will give to thee the keys of the kingdom of Heaven. Feed my lambs, feed my sheep.* (*Matt. xvi; John xxi*)

Q. What do these texts of Scripture prove?

A. That Christ committed to St Peter, and to his lawful successors, the care of His whole flock, that is, of His whole Church, both pastors and people.

Q. Who succeeded to the other apostles?

A. The Bishops of the Holy Catholic Church.

Q. Can the Church err in what it teaches?

A. No; because Christ promised to guide the pastors of His Church, when He said to them, *Going, therefore, teach ye all nations; and behold I am with you all days, even to the consummation of the world.* (*Matt. xxviii. 19, 20*)

Q. Why did Christ promise to remain always with His Church?

A. That He Himself, directing and assisting by His Holy Spirit the pastors of His Church, might teach all ages and nations.

Q. Can the Pope err in his teaching?

A. When, acting as pastor and teacher of all Christians, he defines that a doctrine concerning faith or morals is to be held by the whole Church, he is preserved from error by the guidance of the Holy Ghost.

Q. What do you call that privilege by which the Pope is in certain cases preserved from the possibility of teaching what is not true?

A. It is called the Infallibility of the Pope.

Q. What else did Christ promise to His Church?

A. That the gates of Hell should not prevail against it. (*Matt. xvi. 18*)

Q. What other advantages have we in the True Church?

A. We have true faith with the communion of saints, and the forgiveness of sins. (*Ap. Cr.*)

Q. What means the forgiveness of sins?

A. That Christ left to the pastors of His Church the power of forgiving sins. (*John xx. 23*)

LESSON XII

ON SIN

Wilful	*with consent*
Deed	*an action*
Omission	*something left out*
Contrary	*against*
Disposing	*preparing*
Contemneth	*despises*
Supernatural	*above nature*
Destined	*intended*
Merit	*to deserve*
Repent	*to do penance*
Resolve	*to make a firm purpose*
Amend	*to improve*
Reconcile	*to restore to favour*
Resolution	*firm purpose*
Capital	*chief*
Confession	*a clear humble declaration of our sins to a priest*
Pride	*too high an opinion of one's self*
Recover	*to get back*
Excite	*to stir up*

46

Contrition	bruising of the heart, sorrow for sin
Detest	to hate
Amiable	deserving to be loved
Infinite	without beginning or end; without limit of any kind
Covetousness	too great a desire for riches or gain
Anger	passion
Gluttony	eating or drinking to excess
Envy	uneasiness at another's happiness
Sloth	idleness
Venial	pardonable
Grievous	great or serious

Q. What is sin?

A. Any wilful thought, word, deed, or omission contrary to the law of God.

Q. What is mortal sin?

A. A grievous offence or transgression against the law of God.

Q. Why is it called mortal sin?

A. Because it kills the soul by depriving it of its true life, which is sanctifying grace, and because it brings everlasting death and damnation on the soul.

Q. Does venial sin deprive the soul of sanctifying grace, and deserve everlasting punishment?

A. No; but it hurts the soul by lessening its love for God, and by disposing it to mortal sin: the Scripture says: *he that contemneth small things shall fall by little and little.* (Ecclus. xix. 1)

Q What do you mean by grace?

A. A supernatural gift destined by God for our sanctification, and to enable us to merit Heaven.

Q. What is sanctifying grace?

A. That grace which sanctifies the soul, and makes it pleasing to God.

Q. What is actual grace?

A. It is a supernatural help which God gives us to enable us to resist temptation, avoid sin, and perform good works.

Q. Is grace necessary to salvation?

A. Yes; *Without me*, says Christ, *you can do nothing*. (*John xv.* 5)

Q. Is it a great misfortune to fall into mortal sin?

A. It is the greatest of all misfortunes.

Q. What must we do when we fall into mortal sin?

A. We must repent sincerely, and go to confession as soon as possible.

Q. Why should we go to confession as soon as we fall into mortal sin?

A. That we may recover God's friendship, and be always prepared to die.

Q. What should we do if we cannot go to confession when we fall into mortal sin?

A. We must excite ourselves to perfect contrition, with a sincere desire of going to confession as soon as we can.

Q. How do you express an act of perfect contrition?

A. O my God, I am heartily sorry for having offended Thee, and I detest my sins most sincerely because they displease Thee, my God, who, for Thy infinite goodness and most amiable perfections, art so deserving of all my love; and I firmly purpose by Thy holy grace never more to offend thee and to amend my life.

Q. Will perfect contrition reconcile us to God without confession?

A. Yes; and it is the only means we have to recover God's friendship when we cannot go to confession.

Q. What is necessary for our contrition to be perfect?

A. That we should be truly sorry for our sins, because they are offensive to God, who is so good in Himself, with a sincere resolution not to offend God any more, to satisfy for our sins, and to go to confession as soon as we can.

Q. How many are the chief mortal sins, commonly called capital and deadly sins?

A. Seven: Pride, Covetousness, Lust, Anger, Gluttony, Envy, and Sloth.

Q. Where shall they go who die in mortal sin?

A. To Hell for all eternity.

Q. Where do they go who die in venial sin?

A. To Purgatory.

Indebted	*owing*
Temporary	*lasting for a time*
Correction	*punishment*
Deter	*to frighten*
Relapsing	*falling back*
Atonement	*satisfaction*
Avoid	*to shun*
Commandment	*an order*
Purgatory	*a place for cleansing*

Q. What is Purgatory?

A. A place or state of punishment in the other life, where some souls suffer for a time before they can go to Heaven. (*Matt. xii. 32*)

Q. Do any others go to Purgatory besides those who die in venial sin?

A. Yes; all who die indebted to God's justice on account of mortal sin.

Q. When God forgives mortal sin as to the guilt of it, and the eternal punishment it deserves, does He require temporary punishment to be suffered for it?

A. Yes; very often, and for our correction, to deter us from relapsing into sin, and that we should make some atonement to His offended justice and goodness. (*Num. xiv; II. Kings xii*)

Q. Can the souls in Purgatory be relieved by our prayers and other good works?

A. Yes; being children of God, and still members of the Church, the souls in Purgatory share in the communion of saints, and the Scripture says, *it is a holy and wholesome thought to pray for the dead, that they may be loosed from their sins.* (*Macc. xii. 46*)

Q. What means the communion of saints?

A. It is that union which exists between the members of the three great divisions of the True Church, namely, the faithful on earth, the blessed in Heaven, and the suffering souls in Purgatory.

Q. Do any advantages arise from the communion of saints?

A. Yes; it enables the faithful on earth to assist each other by their prayers and good works, and to be assisted by the prayers of the saints in Heaven; and it enables both the saints in Heaven and the faithful on earth to help the suffering souls in Purgatory.

Q. Is it sufficient for salvation to be members of the True Church?

A. No; we must avoid evil, and do good. (*I. Pet. iii*)

Q. What good shall I do that I may have life everlasting?

A. *If thou wilt enter into life,* says Christ, *keep the Commandments.* (*Matt. xix. 16*)

Q. What Commandments am I to keep?

A. The Ten Commandments of God.

Q. Say the Ten Commandments of God.

A.   1. I am the Lord thy God; thou shalt not have strange
        Gods before me, &c.

2. Thou shalt not take the name of the Lord thy God in
   vain.

3. Remember that thou keep holy the Sabbath day.

4. Honour thy father and thy mother.

5. Thou shalt not kill.

6. Thou shalt not commit adultery.

7. Thou shalt not steal.

8. Thou shalt not bear false witness against thy
   neighbour.

9. Thou shalt not covet thy neighbour's wife.

10. Thou shalt not covet thy neighbour's goods.

     (*Exod. xx*)

**Q. Is it necessary to keep all and every one of the Ten
Commandments?**

A. Yes; the Scripture says, *whosoever shall offend in one is become guilty of all*; that is, the observance of the other commandments will not avail him to salvation. (*James ii. 10*)

Q. Which is the first commandment?

A. I am the Lord thy God; thou shalt not have strange Gods
before me.

Q. What is commanded by the first commandment?

A. To adore one God, and to adore but Him alone.

Q. How are we to adore God?

A. By Faith, Hope, and Charity; by prayer and sacrifice.

Q. What is Faith?

A. A divine virtue by which we firmly believe what God has taught.

Q. How do we know with certainty what God has taught?

A. By the authority of the Church, *which is the pillar and ground of truth.* (*I. Tim. iii. 15*)

Q. Why do we believe what God has taught?

A. Because He is the infallible truth, and therefore cannot deceive nor be deceived.

Q. What is Hope?

A. A divine virtue by which we firmly hope for eternal life, and for the means to obtain it.

Q. Why do we hope in God?

A. Because He is infinitely powerful, good, and merciful, and because He is faithful to His word, and has promised all graces, even Heaven itself, through Jesus Christ, to all those who keep His commandments.

Q. What is Charity?

A. A divine virtue by which we love God above all things for His own sake, and our neighbours as ourselves for the love of God.

Q. Why should we love God above all things for His own sake?

A. Because God alone is infinitely good and perfect.

Q. How are we to love God above all?

A. By loving Him more than ourselves, and more than anything in the world, and by being disposed to sacrifice everything that is most dear to us, even our very lives, if necessary, rather than to offend Him.

Q. Should we often make acts of Faith, Hope, and Charity?

A. Yes; and particularly when we come to the use of reason, and at the hour of death; also, when we are tempted to sin, or have sinned against these divine virtues; and when we prepare ourselves to receive any sacrament.

LESSON XV

ON THE FIRST COMMANDMENT

Endeavouring	*making an effort*
Heretic	*one who, while professing Christianity, holds doctrines condemned by the Church*
Infidel	*one who does not believe in our Lord nor in the Gospel*
Declaration	*making known*
Spiritual	*belonging to the soul*
Edification	*good example*
Motives	*intentions*
Essential	*necessary*
Apostate	*one who falls away from the Church*
Conversion	*turning from bad to good*
Diffidence	*distrust*

54

Q. What is forbidden by the first commandment?

A. All sins against faith, hope, and charity, and other duties of religion.

Q. How does a person sin against faith?

A. By not endeavouring to know what God has taught, by not believing what God has taught, and by not professing his belief in what God has taught.

Q. Who are they who do not endeavour to know what God has taught?

A. Those who neglect to learn the Christian Doctrine.

Q. Who are they who do not believe what God has taught?

A. Heretics and infidels.

Q. Who are they who sin against faith by not professing their belief in what God has taught?

A. All those who by any outward act, profession or declaration, deny the true religion or Church in which they inwardly believe.

Q. Can persons who deny outwardly the true religion or Church, in which they inwardly believe, expect salvation while in that state?

A. No; *Whosoever*, says Christ, *shall deny me before men, I will also deny them before my Father who is in Heaven.* (*Matt. x. 33*)

Q. When, in particular, are we obliged to make open profession of our faith or religion?

A. As often as God's honour, our own spiritual good, or our neighbour's edification requires it. *Whosoever*, says Christ, *shall confess me before men, I will also confess him before my Father who is in Heaven.* (*Matt. x. 32*)

Q. Is a person in the way of salvation who believes in the True Church, and says that in his heart he is attached to it, but who, through pride, human respect, or worldly motives, does not make open profession of it, or does not comply with its essential duties?

A. No; St Paul says, *with the heart we believe unto justice; but with the mouth confession is made unto salvation.* (*Rom. x. 10*)

Q. What does St Paul say of apostates, that is, of those who are fallen away from the true religion or Church?

A. That it is impossible for them to be renewed again to penance; that is, their conversion is extremely difficult.

Q. Why is the conversion of apostates so very difficult?

A. Because by their apostacy they crucify again the Son of God, and make a mockery of Him. (*Heb. vi. 6*)

Q. Which are the sins against hope?

A. Despair and presumption.

Q. What is despair?

A. A diffidence in God's mercy.

Q. What is presumption?

A. A foolish expectation of salvation without making proper use of the necessary means to obtain it.

Q. How does a person sin against the love of God?

A. By every sin, but particularly by mortal sin.

Q. How does a person sin against the love of his neighbour?

A. By injuring him in any respect, and by not assisting him, when able, in his spiritual or corporal necessities.

Images	*representations*
Representations	*likenesses*
Memorials	*things kept in memory*
Incantations	*words said or acts done to injure others through the power of the devil*
Charms	*acts done to do good for ourselves or others through the power of the devil*
Spells	*words said to do good for ourselves or others through the power of the devil*
Superstition	*false devotion*
Omens	*signs of bad or good luck*
Nonsensical	*foolish*
Temples	*dwelling places*
Idolaters	*those who adore false gods*
Communications	*conversations*
Theatrical	*belonging to the theatre*
Ministers	*priests*
Sacred	*holy*
Ceremonies	*outward forms of devotion*
Ridiculed	*laughed at*
Impious	*wicked*
Criminal	*sinful*

Q. What else is forbidden by the first commandment?

A. To give to any creature the honour due to God alone.

Q. Are we forbidden to honour the saints?

A. No; if we only honour them as God's special friends and faithful servants; and if we do not give them supreme or divine honour, which belongs to God alone.

Q. How do Catholics distinguish between the honour they give to God, and the honour they give to the saints, when they pray to God and the saints?

A. Of God alone they beg grace and mercy, and of the saints they only ask the assistance of their prayers. (*Tobias xii. 12*)

Q. Is it lawful to recommend ourselves to the saints and to ask their prayers?

A. Yes; as it is lawful, and a very pious practice, to ask the prayers of our fellow creatures on earth, and to pray for them. (*Thessal. v. 25; James v. 16*)

Q. Why do Catholics kneel before the images of Christ and His saints?

A. To honour Christ and His saints, whom their images represent. (*Exodus xxv*)

Q. Is it proper to show any mark of respect to the crucifix, and to the pictures of Christ and His saints?

A. Yes; because they relate to Christ and His saints, being representations and memorials of them. (*Acts xix. 12; Matt. ix*)

Q. Why do Catholics honour the relics of the saints?

A. Because their bodies have been temples of the Holy Ghost, and at the last day will be honoured and glorified forever in Heaven.

Q. May we, then, pray to the crucifix, or to the image or relics of the saints?

A. By no means; for they have neither life, nor sense, nor power to hear or help us.

Q. Why, then, do we pray before the crucifix, and before the images or relics of the saints?

A. Because they enliven our devotion by exciting pious affections and desires, and by reminding us of Christ and His saints; they also encourage us to imitate their virtues and good works. (*Exodus xxv. 18; John iii. 14*)

Q. Is it not forbidden by the first commandment to make images?

A. No; if we do not make them for gods, to adore and serve them as the idolaters do.

Q. Is there anything else forbidden by the first commandment?

A. Yes; all dealings and communications with the devil; and inquiring, by improper means, after things which are lost, hidden, or to come.

Q. Is it also forbidden to give credit to dreams, to fortune-telling, and the like superstitious practices?

A. Yes; and all incantations, charms, and spells, all superstitious observances of omens and accidents, and such nonsensical remarks are also very sinful.

Q. What do you think of theatrical representations, and other amusements, particularly at wakes, in which religion, its ministers and sacred ceremonies are ridiculed?

A. They are impious and highly criminal, and strictly forbidden by the first commandment.

ON THE SECOND, THIRD, AND FOURTH COMMANDMENTS

Reverence	*veneration, respect*
Oath	*calling God to witness*
Vow	*a solemn promise made to God*
Rash	*hasty*
Cursing	*wishing evil*
Swearing	*taking an oath*
Blasphemy	*speaking badly of God or of holy things*
Servile	*laborious, what is usually done by servants with the bodily powers rather than with those of the mind, and for the good of the body rather than for the good of the mind*
Profane	*to make bad use of holy things*
Defence	*protection*
Superiors	*those placed over us*
Stubbornness	*self-will*
Ill-will	*hatred*
Subjects	*those under authority*
Temporal powers	*those who rule the country*
Station	*employment*
Combine	*to unite together*
Authorities	*those that rule*
Ordinances	*appointment*
Humanity	*kindness*
Reprove	*to check*
Diligent	*careful*

Q. Say the second commandment.

A. Thou shalt not take the name of the Lord thy God in vain.

Q. What is commanded by the second commandment?

A. To speak with reverence of God, and of His saints and ministers; of religion, its practices and ceremonies; and of all things relating to divine service.

Q. What else is commanded by the second commandment?

A. To keep our lawful oaths and vows.

Q. What is forbidden by the second commandment?

A. All false, rash, unjust, and unnecessary oaths; also cursing, swearing, blaspheming, and profane words. (*Matt. v. 34; James v. 12*)

Q. What is an oath?

A. Calling God to be witness that what we say is true, or that we will do what we promise.

Q. Is it ever lawful to swear?

A. It is; when God's honour, our own, or our neighbour's good, or necessary defence, requires it.

Q. What do you mean by an unjust oath?

A. An oath injurious to God, to ourselves, or to our neighbour.

Q. Is a person obliged to keep an unjust oath?

A. No; he sinned in taking it, and would sin also in keeping it.

Q. Is a person obliged to keep a lawful oath?

A. Yes; and it would be perjury to break it.

Q. What is perjury?

A. To break a lawful oath, or to take a false one.

Q. Is perjury a great sin?

A. It is a most grievous sin.

Q. What is a vow?

A. A deliberate promise made to God under pain of sin to do something good or to avoid something displeasing to Him.

Q. Say the third commandment.

A. Remember that thou keep holy the Sabbath day.

Q. What is commanded by the third commandment?

A. To spend the Sunday in prayer and other religious duties.

Q. Which are the chief duties of religion in which we should spend the Sundays?

A. Hearing Mass devoutly is the most important of the religious duties to be performed on Sunday; besides which it would be well to attend vespers or evening devotions, to read good pious books, and, if possible, to go to communion.

Q. Is the hearing of Mass sufficient to sanctify the Sunday?

A. No; a part of the day should also be given to prayer and other good works.

Q. What particular good works are recommended to sanctify the Sunday?

A. The works of mercy, spiritual and corporal, and particularly to instruct the ignorant in the way of salvation, by word and example. (*Daniel xii. 3*)

Q. What is forbidden by the third commandment?

A. All unnecessary servile work, and whatever may hinder the due observance of the Lord's day, or tend to profane it.

Q. Is the sin the greater by being committed on the Lord's Day?

A. Most certainly.

Q. Say the fourth commandment.

A. Honour thy father and thy mother.

Q. What is commanded by the fourth commandment?

A. To love, honour, and obey our parents and superiors. (*Col. iii. 20*)

Q. What is forbidden by the fourth commandment?

A. All contempt, stubbornness, ill-will, and disobedience to parents and superiors.

Q. What are the chief duties of parents?

A. To provide for their children, to instruct them, and all others under their care, in the Christian Doctrine, and such other knowledge as is suitable to their state in life, and by every means in their power to lead them to God. (*I. Tim. v. 8*)

Q. What special reward has God promised to dutiful children?

A. A long and happy life even in this world. (*Ephes. vi*)

Q. What are the duties of subjects to the temporal powers?

A. To be subject to them, and to honour and obey them, not only for wrath, but also for conscience sake, for so is the will of God. (*I. Peter; Romans xiii*)

Q. Does the Scripture require any other duty of subjects?

A. Yes; to pray for kings, and for all who are in high station, that we may lead a quiet and peaceful life. (*I. Tim. ii*)

Q. Is it sinful to resist or combine against the established authorities, or to speak with contempt or disrespect of those who rule over us?

A. Yes; St Paul says, *let every soul be subject to the higher powers; he that resisteth the power resisteth the ordinance of God; and they that resist purchase to themselves damnation.* (*Rom. xiii*)

Q. What are the chief duties of masters to their servants, apprentices, and others under their care?

A. To lead them to God by word and example; to see that they be exact in their religious duties; to treat them with justice and humanity; and to correct and reprove them when necessary.

Q. What does St Paul say to masters?

A. *Masters, do to your servants that which is just and equal, knowing that you also have a Master in Heaven.* (*Col. iv. 1*)

Q. What are the chief duties of servants and apprentices to their masters?

A. To be obedient, respectful, and faithful to them; to be diligent in their work and services; and not to suffer their masters to be injured in their property by any persons.

(Eph. vi; Col. iii)

ON THE FIFTH, SIXTH, SEVENTH, AND EIGHTH COMMANDMENTS

Quarrelling	*noisy, disputing, scolding*
Hatred	*ill-will*
Revenge	*returning evil for evil*
Scandal	*bad example, anything likely to lead others into sin*
Unchaste	*immodest*
Chastity	*purity of body*
Novels	*dangerous stories*
Comedies	*bad plays*
Retain	*to keep back*
Restore	*to give back*
Testimonies	*to give evidence*
Jocose	*merry*
Rash judgement	*forming a bad opinion of another without sufficient grounds*
Backbiting	*speaking with malicious pleasure of the known faults of others in their absence*
Malicious	*intending evil*
Calumny	*accusing our neighbours falsely of something bad*
Detraction	*telling the hidden faults of a neighbour without a just cause when it is likely that we shall injure his character*
Reputation	*good character*

Q. Say the fifth commandment?

A. Thou shalt not kill.

Q. What is forbidden by the fifth commandment?

A. All wilful murder, quarrelling, fighting, hatred, anger, revenge, and drunkenness.

Q. What else is forbidden by the fifth commandment?

A. All injurious words; giving scandal or bad example; and not to ask pardon of those whom we have offended. (*Matt. v. 39*)

Q. Say the sixth commandment.

A. Thou shalt not commit adultery.

Q. What is forbidden by the sixth commandment?

A. All unchaste freedom with another's wife or husband.

Q. What else is forbidden by the sixth commandment?

A. All immodest looks, words, or actions, and everything that is contrary to chastity. (*Col. iii. 5*)

Q. Are immodest songs, discourses, novels, comedies and plays, especially at wakes, forbidden by the sixth commandment?

A. Yes; and it is sinful to join in them, to encourage them, or to be present at them.

Q. Say the seventh commandment.

A. Thou shalt not steal.

Q. What is forbidden by the seventh commandment?

A. All unjust taking or keeping what belongs to another.

Q. What else is forbidden by the seventh commandment?

A. All cheating in buying or selling, or any other injury done to our neighbour in his property. (*I. Cor. v. 10*)

Q. What is commanded by the seventh commandment?

A. To pay our lawful debts, and to give every man his own, and they who retain ill-gotten goods or who have unjustly what belongs to another are obliged to restore them as soon as possible and as far as they are able, otherwise the sin will not be forgiven them.

Q. Say the eighth commandment.

A. Thou shalt not bear false witness against thy neighbour.

Q. What is forbidden by the eighth commandment?

A. All false testimonies, rash judgements, and lies. (*Matt. vii. 1*)

Q. Is it lawful to tell an innocent or jocose lie or to tell a lie for a good purpose?

A. No lie can be lawful or innocent; and no motive, however good, can excuse a lie, because a lie is always sinful and bad in itself. (*John viii. 44*)

Q. What else is forbidden by the eighth commandment?

A. Backbiting, calumny, detraction, and all words and speeches hurtful to our neighbour's honour or reputation.

Q. What is commanded by the eighth commandment?

A. To speak of others with justice and charity, as we would be glad they would speak of us, and to say nothing but the truth.

Q. What must they do who have given false evidence against a neighbour, or who have spoken ill of him or injured his character in any respect?

A. They must repair the injury done him, as far as they are able; and make him satisfaction, by restoring his good name as soon as possible; otherwise the sin will not be forgiven them.

LESSON XIX

ON THE NINTH AND TENTH COMMANDMENTS

Immediate	*near*
Amusements	*plays*
Lascivious	*immodest, improper*
Inflame	*to excite*
Passions	*bad inclinations*
Entertained	*kept in mind*
Deliberately	*with reflection*
Defile	*to make unclean*
Immediate occasions	*things that almost always lead to sin*
Precepts	*commandments*
Calumniate	*to charge falsely and maliciously*
Abstain	*to keep from*

Q. Say the ninth commandment.

A. Thou shalt not covet thy neighbour's wife.

Q. What is forbidden by the ninth commandment?

A. All immodest thoughts and desires, and wilful pleasure in them.

Q. What else is forbidden by the ninth commandment?

A. All immediate occasions of immodest thoughts and desires.

Q. What are the immediate occasions of immodest thoughts and desires?

A. Unchaste words and discourses, immodest books and pictures, and all amusements dangerous to charity.

Q. What else may be deemed immediate occasions of immodest thoughts and desires?

A. Lascivious looks and touches, idleness, bad company, all excess in eating and drinking, and whatever tends to inflame the passions.

Q. Is it sinful to have unchaste thoughts, where there is no intention or desire to indulge them by any criminal action?

A. They are always very dangerous, and when entertained deliberately and with pleasure, they defile the soul like criminal actions. (*Matt. v. 28*)

Q. Say the tenth commandment.

A. Thou shalt not covet thy neighbour's goods.

Q. What is forbidden by the tenth commandment?

A. All covetous thoughts and unjust desires of our neighbour's goods or profits.

Q. To how many commandments may the ten command-ments be reduced?

A. To these two principal commandments which are the two great precepts of charity: – *Thou shalt love the Lord thy God with thy whole heart, and with thy whole soul, and with all thy strength, and with all thy mind, and thy neighbour as thyself: This do and thou shalt live.* (*Luke x; Mark xii*)

Q. And who is my neighbour?

A. Mankind of every description, and without any excep-tion of persons, even those who injure us, or differ from us in religion. (*Luke x. 29*)

Q. How am I to love my neighbour as myself?

A. *As you would,* says Christ, *that men should do to you do you also to them in like manner.* (*Luke iv. 31*)

Q. What particular duties are required of me by that rule?

A. Never to injure your neighbour by word or deed, in his person, property, or character; always to wish well to him, and to pray for him, and to assist him, as far as you are able, in his spiritual and corporal necessities.

Q. Am I also obliged to love my enemies?

A. Most certainly – *Love your enemies,* says Christ, *do good to them that hate you, bless them that curse you, and pray for them that persecute and calumniate you.* (*Luke vi: Matt. v.*)

Inclusive	*including both*
Solemnise	*to celebrate with Nuptial Mass, the Nuptial Blessing and with much pomp*
Kindred	*relationship*
Prohibited	*forbidden*
Clandestine	*secret*
Culpable	*blameable*
Mortify	*to cause suffering*
Appetite	*bad desires*
Commemoration	*remembrance*

Q. Are there any other commandments besides the ten commandments of God?

A. Yes; the commandments or precepts of the Church, which are chiefly six.

Q. Say the six commandments of the Church.

A. 1. To hear Mass on Sundays and all holy days of obligation.

2. To fast and abstain on the days commanded.

3. To confess our sins at least once a year.

4. To receive worthily the Blessed Eucharist at Easter, or within the time appointed: that is, from Ash Wednesday to the octave-day of SS Peter and Paul inclusive.

5. To contribute to the support of our pastors.

6. Not to solemnise marriage at the forbidden times, not to marry persons within the forbidden degrees of kindred, or otherwise prohibited by the Church; nor clandestinely.

Q. What are our first and chief duties on Sundays and kept holy days?

A. To hear Mass devoutedly; and in every other respect to keep them holy.

Q. Is it a mortal sin not to hear Mass on a Sunday or kept holy day?

A. It is, if the omission be culpable; and fathers and mothers, masters and mistresses, and all such persons sin grievously, if without sufficient cause, they hinder children, servants, or any others subject to them from hearing Mass on a Sunday or kept holy day. (*Il. Thes. iii. 4, 14*)

Q. What do you mean by holy days?

A. Certain solemn days ordered by the Church to be kept holy.

Q. Why were holy days instituted by the Church?

A. To recall to our minds, with praise and thanksgiving, the great mysteries of religion, and the virtues and rewards of the saints, and that we might glorify God on them.

Q. How are we to keep holy days?

A. As we should keep Sundays.

Q. What are we obliged to do by the second commandment of the Church?

A. To give part of the year to fasting and abstinence. (*Matt. vi. 16, 17, 18*)

✝

Q. What do you mean by fast days?

A. Certain days on which we are allowed but one meal, and forbidden flesh meat.

Q. What do you mean by days of abstinence?

A. Certain days on which we are forbidden to eat flesh meat, but are allowed the usual number of meals.

Q. Why does the Church command us to fast and abstain?

A. To mortify our sinful passions and appetites, and to satisfy our sins by doing penance for them.

Q. Why does the Church command us to abstain from flesh meat on Fridays?

A. In honour and commemoration of our Saviour's death.

LESSON XXI

THE PRECEPTS OF THE CHURCH *(continued)*

Penalties	*punishments*
Sacrilege	*profaning holy things, persons or places*
Valid	*having force or strength, a valid marriage is one by which the parties are, before God, bound to one another as husband and wife*
Discern	*to distinguish*
Decree	*a law*
Excluded	*shut out*
Council	*an assembly of Bishops*
Null	*of no effect*
Heathen	*an idolater*
Publican	*a tax gatherer in the old law*

Q. What means the commandment of confessing, our sins at least once a year?

A. It means that we are bound under pain of mortal sin to go to confession at least once within the year, and that we are threatened with very severe penalties by the Church if we neglect doing so.

Q. Does a bad confession satisfy the obligation of confessing our sins once a year?

A. So far from it that it renders us more guilty by the additional crime of sacrilege.

Q. Is it sufficient to go but once a year to confession?

A. No; frequent confession is necessary for all those who fall into mortal sin, or who desire to advance in virtue.

Q. At what age are children obliged to go to confession?

A. As soon as they are capable of committing sin; that is, when they come to the use of reason, which is generally supposed to be about the age of seven years.

Q. Where, and from whom, are we to receive the Blessed Eucharist at Easter?

A. In our own parish, and from our own pastor, or elsewhere with his leave.

Q. At what age are children obliged to receive the Blessed Eucharist?

A. As soon as they are able to discern the body of the Lord; that is, when they understand what the Blessed Eucharist is, and how they should be prepared to receive it worthily. (*I. Cor. xi. 29*)

Q. What punishment has the Church decreed against those who neglect to receive the Blessed Eucharist at Easter?

A. They are to be excluded from the house of God whilst living, and deprived of Christian burial when they die. *(Fourth Council of Lateran, Can. 21)*

Q. Are we obliged in conscience and justice to contribute to the support of our pastors?

A. Yes; and by a divine precept also. St Paul says: *So the Lord ordained, that they who preach the Gospel should live by the Gospel (I. Cor. ix. 13, 14)*

Q. What is a clandestine marriage?

A. Every marriage of Catholics is declared clandestine by the Church, at which the Parish Priest of the place where the ceremony is gone through is not present, or another priest, by his leave, or by leave of the Bishop, with two or three witnesses. *(Law of 1907)*

Q. Is a clandestine marriage a lawful and good marriage?

A. A clandestine marriage is no marriage; it is null and void in the sight of God and of His Church.

Q. Do the precepts of the Church oblige under pain of mortal sin?

A. Yes; *he that will not hear the Church,* says Christ, *let him be to thee as the heathen and the publican.* *(Luke x. 16; Matt. xviii. 17)*

Q. What is necessary to keep the commandments of God and of His Church?

A. The grace of God, which is to be obtained chiefly by prayer and the sacraments.

LESSON XXII

ON PRAYER

Elevation	*a raising up*
Petition	*a request*
Necessaries	*wants*
Affliction	*great troubles*
Posture	*position*
Acceptable	*agreeable*
Contrite	*sorrowful*
Fervour	*earnestness*
Perseverance	*continuance*
Resignation	*submission*
Distraction	*wandering of the mind*
Abomination	*something hateful*
Beneficial	*of benefit*

Q. What is prayer?

A. An elevation of the soul to God; to adore Him, to bless His holy name, to praise His goodness, and return Him thanks for His benefits.

Q. Is prayer anything else?

A. Yes; it is a humble petition to God for all necessaries for soul and body.

Q. When should we pray?

A. Christ Himself says, *we ought always to pray*. (*Luke xviii. 1*)

77

Q. How can we always pray?

A. By offering to God all our thoughts, words, and actions; by keeping ourselves in the state of grace, and by praying at certain times.

Q. At what particular times should we pray?

A. On Sundays and holy days, every morning and every night, and in all dangers, temptations, and afflictions.

Q. After what manner should we pray?

A. With all possible attention and devotion, and in a respectful posture on bended knees.

Q. What conditions are necessary to render our prayers acceptable?

A. We must always offer them with a humble and contrite heart; with fervour and perseverance; with confidence in God's goodness; with resignation to His will, and in the name of Jesus Christ.

Q. What do you say to those who, at their prayers, think not of God, nor of what they say?

A. If their distractions be wilful, their prayers, instead of pleasing God, offend Him, and are an abomination to Him. (*Matt. xv. 8*)

Q. What prayers are most recommended to us?

A. The Lord's Prayer, the Hail Mary, the Apostles' Creed, and the Confiteor or General Confession.

Q. Does the Church also recommend the Acts of Faith, Hope and Charity?

A. Yes; most certainly; they are an excellent form of prayer, and remind us of our chief duties to God.

Q. What are our chief duties to God?

A. To believe in Him, to hope in Him, and to love Him.

Q. Why do you make an Act of Contrition before the Acts of Faith, Hope, and Charity?

A. To obtain pardon of my sins, and thereby to render my prayers more acceptable to God, and more beneficial to myself.

LESSON XXIII

ON THE LORD'S PRAYER AND HAIL MARY

Hallowed	*praised*
Trespasses	*offences*
Intercession	*prayers for others*
Instituted	*established*
Baptism	*washing*
Confirmation	*strengthening*
Extreme Unction	*last anointing*

Q. Who made the Lord's Prayer?

A. Jesus Christ. *(Matt. vi. 9, 10)*

Q; Whom do you call *Our Father*, when you say the Lord's Prayer?

A. Almighty God, who is the common Father of all.

79

Q. What means, *Hallowed be thy name*?

A. By this we beg that God's name may be praised and glorified by all His creatures.

Q. What means, *Thy kingdom come*?

A. By this we beg that God may reign in our hearts by His grace, in this life, and that we may reign forever with Him in the next.

Q. What means, *Thy will be done*?

A. By this we beg that God would enable us by His grace, to do His will in all things on earth, as the angels and saints do in Heaven.

Q. What means, *Give us this day our daily bread*?

A. By this we beg for all necessaries for our souls and bodies.

Q. What means, *Forgive us our trespasses, as we forgive them who trespass against us*?

A. By this we beg that God would forgive us our offences, as we forgive them who offend us.

Q. Will God forgive us our offences if we do not forgive our enemies, and all those who have offended us?

A. No; God will show no mercy to us, unless we forgive from our hearts our enemies, and all those who have offended or injured us. (*Matt. xviii. 35; vi. 15*)

Q. What means, *Lead us not into temptation*?

A. By this we beg that God would strengthen us against all temptations.

Q. What means, *Deliver us from Evil*?

A. By this we beg that God would deliver us, in body and soul, from all evil, particularly that of sin.

Q. Who made the Hail Mary?

A. The Angel Gabriel and St Elizabeth, made the first part of it, and the Church made the last. (*Luke i. 28*)

Q. Is it lawful to honour the Virgin Mary?

A. Yes; whereas God Himself so much honoured her; and the Scripture says, *All nations shall call her blessed*. (*Luke i. 48*)

Q. What honour do we give our Blessed Lady?

A. We honour her more than all the other saints, because she is the Mother of God; but we never give her divine or supreme honour, which is due to God alone.

Q. Why do Catholics so often repeat the Hail Mary and the Holy Mary?

A. To honour the mystery of the Incarnation, which that prayer expresses; and to show their great respect and devotion to the Mother of God; and their special confidence in her assistance, particularly at the hour of death.

Q. And why do you always say the Hail Mary after the Lord's Prayer?

A. That by her intercession we may more easily obtain what we ask for in the Lord's Prayer.

ON THE SACRAMENTS IN GENERAL, AND ON BAPTISM

Administration	*the act of giving*
Matrimony	*marriage*
Heirs	*those who have a claim by descent*
Remit	*to forgive*
Actual	*what we do ourselves*
Layman	*one not in holy orders*
Renounce	*to give up*
Pomps	*vanities of the world*

Q. By what other means besides prayer can we obtain the grace of God?

A. By the sacraments, which are the most powerful of all means.

Q. What is a sacrament?

A. A sensible sign or action instituted by Christ to give grace.

Q. Whence have the sacraments the power of giving grace?

A. From the merits of Christ, which they apply to our souls.

Q. Why are so many ceremonies used in the administration of the sacraments?

A. To excite devotion and reverence to them, and to signify and explain their effects.

Q. How many sacraments are there?

A. Seven: Baptism, Confirmation, Eucharist, Penance, Extreme Unction, Holy Orders, and Matrimony. (*Council of Trent, Sess. vii. c. 1*)

Q. What is Baptism?

A. A sacrament which cleanses us from original sin, makes us Christians and children of God, and heirs to the kingdom of Heaven.

Q. Does Baptism also remit the actual sins committed before it?

A. Yes; and all punishments due to them.

Q. Is Baptism necessary to salvation?

A. Yes; without it we cannot enter into the kingdom of God. (*John iii. 5*)

Q. Who are appointed by Christ to give Baptism?

A. The pastors of His Church; but in case of necessity any layman or woman can give it.

Q. How is Baptism given?

A. By pouring water on the head of the person to be baptised, saying at the same time, *I baptise thee in the name of the Father, and of the Son, and of the Holy Ghost.* (*Matt. xxviii. 19*)

Q. What do we promise in Baptism?

A. To renounce the devil, with all his works and pomps.

ON CONFIRMATION

Imposition	laying on
Special	particular
Wisdom	power to judge rightly
Counsel	advice
Fortitude	courage
Obligations	duties
Morals	manners

Q What is Confirmation?

A. A sacrament which makes us strong and perfect Christians.

Q. How does the bishop give Confirmation?

A. By the imposition of hands, and by prayer, that is, he holds out his hands, and prays at the same time that the Holy Ghost may descend upon those who are to be confirmed; and then makes the sign of the cross on their foreheads with chrism. (*Acts viii. 15, 17*)

Q. Why does the bishop give the person he confirms a stroke on the cheek?

A. To put. them in mind that by Confirmation they are strengthened to suffer; and if necessary, even to die for Christ.

Q. To receive confirmation worthily, is it necessary to be in the state of grace?

A. Yes: and children of an age to learn should be instructed in the Christian Doctrine.

Q. What special preparation should be made for Confirmation?

A. To make a good confession, and by fervent prayer to beseech your Heavenly Father to send His Holy Spirit on you. (*Luke xi. 13*)

Q. What do you think of those who receive Confirmation in the state of mortal sin?

A. They receive no benefit by it, but become more sinful by adding to their former guilt the horrid crime of sacrilege.

Q. What graces are received by Confirmation?

A. The seven gifts of the Holy Ghost.

Q. Repeat the seven gifts of the Holy Ghost.

A. Wisdom, Understanding, Counsel, Fortitude, Knowledge, Piety, and the Fear of the Lord.

Q. What obligations do we contract by Confirmation?

A. To profess our faith openly; not to deny our religion on any occasion whatsoever; and, like good soldiers of Christ, to be faithful to Him unto death. (*Apoc. ii. 10*)

Q. Is it a great sin to neglect Confirmation?

A. Yes; especially in these evil days, when faith and morals are exposed to so many and such violent temptations.

On the Blessed Eucharist

Divinity	*Godhead*
Priest	*one who offers sacrifice*
Victim	*what is offered in sacrifice and destroyed*
Reserved	*kept back*
Consecration	*making sacred*
Figures	*representations*
Interior	*within, belonging to the mind*
Recollection	*attention to God*
Remembrance	*memory*
Ends	*purposes, intentions*

Q. What is the Blessed Eucharist?

A. The sacrament of the body and blood, soul and divinity, of Jesus Christ, under the appearances of bread and wine.

Q. What means the word *Eucharist*?

A. A special grace or gift of God; and it means, also, a solemn act of thanksgiving to God for all His mercies.

Q. What do you mean by the appearances of bread and wine?

A. The taste, colour, and form of bread and wine, which still remain after the substance of the bread and wine has been changed into the body and blood of Christ.

Q. Are both the body and blood of Christ under the appearance of bread and under the appearance of wine?

A. Yes; Christ is whole and entire, true God and true man, under the appearance of each.

Q. Are we to believe that the God of all glory is under the appearance of our corporal food?

A. Yes; as we must also believe that the same God of all glory suffered death under the appearance of a criminal on the cross.

Q. How can the bread and wine become the body and blood of Christ?

A. By the goodness and power of God, with whom no work shall be impossible. (*Luke i. 37*)

Q. Are we assured that Christ changed bread and wine into His body and blood?

A. Yes; by the very words which Christ Himself said, when He instituted the Blessed Eucharist at His last supper.

Q. Which are the words Christ said when He instituted the Blessed Eucharist?

A. *This is my body, this is my blood.* (*Matt. xxvi. 26, 28*)

Q. Did Christ give power to the priests of His Church to change bread and wine into His body and blood?

A. Yes; when He said to His apostles at His last supper, *do this for a commemoration of me.* (*Luke xxii. 19*)

Q. Why did Christ give to the priests of His Church so great a power?

A. That His children throughout all ages and all nations might have a most acceptable sacrifice to offer to their Heavenly Father, and the most precious food to nourish their souls.

Q. What is a sacrifice?

A. An offering to God alone by a lawful priest of some sensible thing which is destroyed, to give God supreme honour, to thank Him for His benefits, to obtain pardon of our sins, and all other graces and blessings, through Jesus Christ.

Q. What is the sacrifice of the New Law?

A. The Mass.

Q. What is the Mass?

A. The sacrifice of the body and blood of Christ, which are really present under the appearance of bread and wine, and are offered to God by the priest for the living and the dead.

Q. Is the Mass a different sacrifice from that of the cross?

A. No; because the same Christ who once offered Himself a bleeding victim to His Heavenly Father on the cross continues to offer Himself in an unbloody manner, by the hands of His priests on our altars.

Q. Was the Mass offered in the Old Law?

A. No; so great a sacrifice was reserved for the New Law, which was to fulfil the figures of the Old Law, and to give religion its full perfection.

Q. At what part of the Mass are the bread and wine changed into the body and blood of Christ?

A. At the consecration.

Q. By whom are the bread and wine changed into the body and blood of Christ?

A. By the priest, but it is by the power of the words of Christ, whose person the priest represents at the awful moment of consecration.

Q. What are the ends for which Mass is said?

A. To give God honour and glory, to thank Him for His benefits, to obtain the pardon of our sins, and all other graces and blessings, through Jesus Christ.

Q. For what other end is Mass offered?

A. To continue and represent the sacrifice of Christ on the cross. *This do*, says Christ, *for a commemoration of me*. (I. Cor. xi. 25)

Q. How should we assist at Mass?

A. With great interior recollection and piety, and with every mark of outward respect and devotion.

Q. Which is the best manner of hearing Mass?

A To offer it to God with the priest for the same purpose for which it is said; to meditate on Christ's sufferings, and go to communion.

Lesson XXVII
On Communion and Penance

Conduce	*to lead to*
Lively	*active*
Ardent	*burning*
Banquet	*a feast*
Exterior	*the outside*
Meditation	*thinking*

Q. What do you mean by going to communion?

A. Receiving the Blessed Eucharist.

Q. Is it advisable to go often to communion?

A. It is, as nothing can conduce more to a holy life. *He that eateth of this bread*, says Christ, *shall live forever*. (*John vi. 59*)

Q. How must we be prepared for communion?

A. We must be in a state of grace, we must have a lively faith, a firm hope, and an ardent charity. (*I. Cor. xi. 28*)

Q. What means to be in a state of grace?

A. To be free at least from the guilt of mortal sin.

Q. How are we to live a lively faith?

A. By firmly believing that the Blessed Eucharist which we are about to receive is Jesus Christ Himself, true God and true man, His very flesh and blood, with His soul and divinity.

Q. How are we to have a firm hope?

A. By having a great confidence in the goodness of Christ, who gives Himself to us without reserve in this banquet of His love.

Q. And how are we to have an ardent charity?

A. By returning love for love to Christ, and by devoting ourselves in earnest to His service all the days of our lives.

Q. Is anything else required before communion?

A. Yes; to be fasting from midnight, and we should appear very modest and humble, and clean in dress, showing in our whole exterior the greatest devotion and reverence to so holy a sacrament.

Q. What should we do after communion?

A. We should spend some time in meditation and prayer, and particularly in acts of thanksgiving.

Q. Is it a great sin to receive it unworthily?

A. Yes; *Whosoever receives unworthily shall be guilty of the body and blood of the Lord, and eats Judgement; that is, damnation to himself, not discerning the body of the Lord.* (I. Cor. xi. 27, 29)

Q. What do you mean by receiving unworthily?

A. To receive the Blessed Eucharist in the state of mortal sin.

Q. What should a person do if he be in mortal sin before communion?

A. He must obtain pardon in the sacrament of penance.

Q. What is penance?

A. A sacrament by which the sins are forgiven which are committed after baptism.

Q. By whose power are sins forgiven?

A. By the power of God, which Christ left to the pastors of His Church.

Q. When did Christ leave to the pastors of His Church the power of forgiving sins?

A. Chiefly when He said to His apostles: – *Receive ye the Holy Ghost; whose sins you shall forgive, they are forgiven them; and whose sins you shall retain, they are retained.* (*John xx.* 22, 23)

Q. What must we do to obtain pardon for our sins in the sacrament of penance?

A. We must make a good confession.

LESSON XXVIII

ON CONFESSION AND INDULGENCES

Predominant	*chief*
Detestation	*hatred*
Ingratitude	*unthankfulness*
Accuse	*to charge*
Renew	*to make new*
Absolution	*forgiveness*
Conceal	*to hide*
Incur	*to deserve*
Penitents	*those who confess with sorrow*
Indulgence	*a favour*
Canonical	*appointed by the canons or laws of the Church*
Cancelled	*blotted out*
Licence	*liberty*

Insufficiency	*want of power*
Superabundant	*more than enough*
Compliance	*performances*
Prescribes	*appoints*
Promote	*to encourage*
Amendment	*improvement*

Q. Which is the best method to prepare for a good confession?

A. First, earnestly beg of God the grace to make a good confession; secondly to examine ourselves carefully on the commandments of God and of His Church; on the seven deadly sins; and particularly on our predominant passion, and the duties of our station in life; that we may know in what, and how often, we have sinned by thought, word, deed, or omission; thirdly, to make Acts of Faith, Hope, and Charity; and fourthly, to excite ourselves to a sincere contrition for our sins.

Q. What is contrition?

A. A hearty sorrow and detestation of sin for having offended God, with a firm resolution of sinning no more.

Q. How may we excite ourselves to contrition?

A. By the following motives or considerations:
The fear of Hell; the loss of Heaven; our ingratitude in offending God, who is so good to us; and the injury our sins do to God who is infinitely good in Himself.

Q. Do you recommend any other motive to excite sorrow for our sins?

A. Yes; to consider that the Son of God died for our sins, and that we crucify Him again as often as we offend Him.

Q. Which of these motives is the best to excite contrition?

A. To be sorry for our sins, because they are offensive to God, who is infinitely good and perfect in Himself.

Q. What must we do at confession?

A. We must beg the priest's blessing, say the Confiteor, accuse ourselves of our sins, listen attentively to his instructions and renew our sorrow when he gives absolution.

Q. What do you think of those who conceal a mortal sin in confession?

A. They commit a most grievous sin by telling a lie to the Holy Ghost; and instead of obtaining pardon they incur much more the wrath of God. (*Acts v*)

Q. What must persons do who did not carefully examine their consciences or who had not sincere sorrow for their sins, or who willingly concealed a mortal sin in confession?

A They must truly repent of all such bad and sacrilegious confessions, and make them all over again.

Q. What is the surest sign that our confessions were good, and that we had sincere sorrow for our sins?

A. The amendment of our lives.

Q. What should we do after confession?

A. We should return God thanks, and diligently perform the penance enjoined by the confessor.

Q. What do you mean by the penance enjoined by the confessor?

A. The prayers and other good works which he enjoins on penitents, in satisfaction for their sins.

Q. Will the penance enjoined in confession always satisfy for our sins?

A. No; but whatever else is wanting may be supplied by indulgences, and by our own penitential endeavours.

Q. What does the Church teach concerning indulgences?

A. That Christ gave power to the Church to grant indulgences, and that they are most useful to Christian people. (*Council of Trent, Sess. xxv*)

Q. What is the use of an indulgence?

A. It releases from canonical penances, enjoined by the Church on penitents, for certain sins.

Q. Has an indulgence any other effect?

A. It also remits the temporary punishment with which God often visits our sins, and which must be suffered in this life or in the next, unless cancelled by indulgences, or by acts of penance, or other good works.

Q. Has the Church the power to grant such indulgences?

A. *Yes; whatsoever*, says Christ to St Peter, *thou shalt loose upon earth, it shall be loosed also in Heaven*. (*Matt. xvi. 19; II. Cor. ii. 10*)

Q. To whom does the Church grant indulgences?

A. To such only as are in the state of grace, and are sincerely desirous to amend their lives, and to satisfy God's justice by penitential works.

Q. Is an indulgence a pardon for sins to come or a licence to commit sin?

A. No; nor can it remit past sins; for sin must be remitted by penance, as to the guilt of it, and as to the eternal punishment due to mortal sin, before an indulgence can be gained.

Q. Why does the Church grant indulgences?

A. To assist our weakness, and to supply our insufficiency in satisfying the divine justice for our transgressions.

Q. When the Church grants indulgences, what does it offer God to supply our weakness and insufficiency, and in satisfaction for our sins?

A. The merits of Christ, which are infinite and superabundant, together with the virtues and good works of His Virgin Mother, and of all His saints.

Q. What conditions are generally necessary to gain indulgences?

A. A good confession and communion, and a faithful compliance with the other good works which the Church requires on such occasions.

Q. What are the other good works which the Church usually prescribes in order to gain indulgences?

A. Prayer, fasting, and alms-deeds, which good works, besides confession and communion, indulgences promote; and on this account also, they are most useful to Christian people.

Resigned	submissive
Inferior	lower
Intention	motive
Effaced	blotted out
Bliss	happiness
Majesty	grandeur of a king
Providence	God's care of all things
Prosper	to succeed

Q. What is Extreme Unction?

A. A sacrament which gives grace to die well; and which was instituted chiefly for the spiritual strength and comfort of dying persons.

Q. Is Extreme Unction given to all persons in danger of death?

A. No; only to such as are in danger of death by sickness.

Q. How should we prepare ourselves for Extreme Unction?

A. By a good confession, and we should be truly sorry for our sins, and resigned to the will of God, when we are receiving the last sacrament.

Q. Who are appointed to administer the sacrament of Extreme Unction?

A. The priests of the Church, as St James teaches; and, so the Church has constantly practised. (*James v. 14, 1*)

Q. What is Holy Orders?

A. A sacrament which gives bishops, priests, and inferior clergy to the Church, and enables them to perform their several duties in it.

Q. What is Matrimony?

A. A sacrament which gives grace to the husband and wife to live happy together, and to bring up their children in the fear and love of God. (*Matt. xix. 6*)

Q. Do they receive the grace of the sacrament of matrimony, who contract marriage in the state of mortal sin?

A. No; they are guilty of a very great sacrilege, by profaning so great a sacrament; and instead of a blessing, they receive their condemnation. (*Eph. v. 32*)

Q. What should persons do to receive worthily the sacrament of marriage?

A. They should make a good confession, and earnestly beseech God to grant them a pure intention; and to direct them in the choice they are to make.

Q. Should children consult their parents on their intended marriage?

A. Yes; and be advised by them according to reason and religion – they should also give timely notice to their pastors.

Q. What is the reason so many marriages prove unhappy?

A. Because many enter into that holy state from unworthy motives, and with guilty consciences; therefore their marriages are not blessed by God.

Q. Can the bond or tie of marriage be ever broken?

A. It never can, but by the death of the husband or wife. *(Matt. xix.; Rom. vii.; I.. Cor. vii)*

Q. Can the sacraments be received more than once?

A. All can, except Baptism, Confirmation, and Holy Orders, which imprint on the soul a character or spiritual mark which can never be effaced.

Q. Which sacraments are most necessary for us?

A. Baptism and Penance.

Q. Why did Christ institute the sacraments?

A. For the sanctification of our souls, and to prepare us for a happy and glorious resurrection.

Q. What means the resurrection of the body?

A. That we shall all rise again on the last day, with the same bodies which we had in this life.

Q. What do you mean by the last day?

A. The day of general judgement; when we must all appear before the judgement seat of Christ; and then He will render to every one according to his works. (*II. Cor. v. 10; Matt. xvi. 27*)

Q. Will our bodies rise united to our souls?

A. Yes; to share in the soul's eternal bliss or misery.

Q. How are the bodies of the saints to rise?

A. Glorious and immortal.

Q. Are the bodies of the damned to rise glorious?

A. No; but they shall rise immortal, to live forever in eternal flames.

Q. In what manner will Christ come to judge us?

A. In the clouds of Heaven, with great power and majesty, and all the angels with Him. (*Matt. xxiv. 30; xxv. 31*)

Q. As everyone is judged immediately after death, what need is there of a general judgement?

A. That the providence of God, which often here permits the good to suffer, and the wicked to prosper, may appear just before all men.

Q. What will Christ say to the good on the last day?

A. *Come, ye blessed of my Father, possess the kingdom prepared for you.* (Matt. xxv. 34)

Q. What will Christ say to the wicked on the last day?

A. *Depart from me, ye cursed, into everlasting fire, which was prepared for the devil and his angels.* (Matt. xxv. 41)

Q. Where must the wicked go at the last day?

A. They shall go, both body and soul, into everlasting punishment. (Matt. xxv. 46)

Q. And where will the just go at the last day?

A. The just will enter, with glorious and immortal bodies, into life everlasting. (Matt. xxv. 46)

Q. What means life everlasting?

A. It means that if we serve God faithfully in this life, we shall be happy with Him forever in Heaven.

Q. What is the happiness of Heaven?

A. To see, love, and enjoy God in the kingdom of His glory forever and ever. *Amen.*

Q. What means *Amen*?

A. So be it.

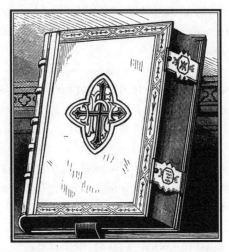

Q. Does God require us to believe things we cannot understand?

A. Yes; when we have His authority that they are true.

Q. Why must we believe mysteries of religion?

A. Because we have God's word that they are true.

Q. How many mysteries of religion are there?

A. There are several mysteries of religion, but of these there are five which are called principal mysteries.

Q. Are these five principal mysteries more necessary to be believed than the others?

A. No; it is just as necessary to believe all the other mysteries of religion, for we have God's word for the others as well as for the five.

Q. Is it more necessary that they should be explicitly believed?

A. It is; for without a substantial knowledge of these five mysteries no one who has come to the use of reason can be saved, whereas a knowledge of other mysteries is not always necessary. We must believe all of them, we need know only some.

Q. What are those things which are absolutely necessary to be known by everyone who has come to the use of reason?

A. First, that there is only one God; second, that there are three Persons in God – the Father, the Son, and the Holy Ghost; thirdly, that God the Son, the second Person, became man for us, that He was crucified, died, and rose again; fourthly, that God rewards good and punishes evil.

Q. Besides these things, is there anything else necessary to be known by all who have an opportunity of learning?

A. Yes; every Christian who can, is bound under pain of sin to know at least in substance, (1) the Lord's Prayer, (2) the Hail Mary, (3) the Apostles' Creed, (4) the Commandments of God and of the Church, (5) the sacraments, or at least those of them which each Christian must receive, and (6) the duties of each one's state in life.

Q. How are we made partakers of the sin and punishment of our first parents?

A. We are made partakers of their sin by being conceived and born in original sin, that is, without grace, which they by their sin lost to themselves as well as to us, and we partake of their punishments by being subject to death and the various sufferings of this life.

Q. How many kinds of sin are there?

A. Two – original and actual.

Q. How is actual sin divided?

A. Into mortal and venial sin.

Q. How many kinds of mortal sin?

A. Seven – Pride, &c.

Q. What is necessary to constitute a mortal sin?

A. Grievous matter, perfect knowledge, and full consent.

Q. How many ways of committing sin?

A. Four – thought, word, deed, and omission.

Q. What is venial sin?

A. That which lessens, but does not entirely take away, the grace of God from our souls.

Q. How many venial sins would be a mortal sin?

A. No amount of them.

Q. How do you know there is such a place in the other life as Purgatory?

A. I am sure there is, because the Catholic Church, which I know to be infallible, has always taught it; and besides, the Scripture says, *it is a holy and wholesome thought to pray for the dead that they may be loosed from their sins*. Now, if there were no place in the other life but Heaven and Hell, it could not be either a holy or a wholesome thought to pray for the dead. There would be no use in praying for them in Heaven, they would not want our prayers, they are already enjoying the sight of God, and are therefore as happy as they can be; nor would there be any use in praying for those in Hell (out of Hell there is no redemption); but, as there are among the dead some persons for whom it is a holy and a wholesome thought to pray, these persons must be in some other place or state besides Heaven or Hell, and that other place or state we call Purgatory.

Q. By what sins are the commandments broken?

A. By all sins.

Q. When did God give the commandments to the Israelites?

A. In the year of the world, 2513; before Christ, 1491.

Q. What is this law called?

A. The written law, because it was written on two tables of stone.

Q. Had they no law before that?

A. They had the law of nature – that is, reason and conscience.

Q. What law followed the written law?

A. The law of grace, which will last till the end of time.

Q. Is any portion of the Old Law still in force?

A. Yes; the Ten Commandments.

Q. Were there sacraments before the time of Christ?

A. Yes; the Sacraments of the Old Law, but they did not confer grace.

Q. What were they?

A. Circumcision, the Paschal Lamb, and a great number of purifications.

Q. What became of these Sacraments?

A. They ceased at the time of Jesus Christ.

Q. What Sacraments did Jesus Christ substitute for them?

A. The Sacraments of the New Law.

Q. How many things are necessary to constitute a sacrament?

A. Three; there must be a sensible sign; it must be instituted by Christ, and it must give grace.

Q. Could anyone but God institute a sacrament?

A. No; for no one could give interior grace to an outward sign but God.

Q. Which are the sacraments of the dead?

A. Baptism and Penance.

Q. Why are they called sacraments of the dead?

A. Because they raise the soul from the death of sin to the life of grace.

Q. Have both these sacraments always this effect?

A. If received with proper dispositions Baptism always has, but Penance has not, for it is often received by persons whose souls are not dead in sin. In this case, however, it increases grace in the soul.

Q. What dispositions are necessary on the part of an adult receiving Baptism?

A. He must have faith and sorrow for his actual mortal sins, and if he receives Baptism without these dispositions, it will not forgive either his original sin or his actual sins.

Q. Must he then be baptised again in order to obtain forgiveness of these sins when Baptism was received without the proper dispositions?

A. No; Baptism cannot be received a second time, but the moment he has the dispositions which he ought to have had at the time of his Baptism, the Sacrament, already received, produces its effect. If, however, he falls into another mortal sin between the time of his Baptism and the time he gets into the required dispositions, it will also be necessary for him to get forgiveness of such sin in the sacrament of Penance or by perfect contrition.

Q. Which are the sacraments of the living?

A. Confirmation, the Blessed Eucharist, Extreme Unction, Holy Orders, and Matrimony.

Q. Why are they called sacraments of the living?

A. Because we must be in the state of grace to receive them.

Q. How many sacraments give the character?

A. Three – Baptism, Confirmation, and Holy Orders. Baptism gives the character of a Christian. Confirmation, the character of a perfect Christian. Holy Orders, the character of the priesthood.

Q. In what sacraments is anointing used?

A. In Baptism, Confirmation, Extreme Unction, and Holy Orders.

Q. What is the matter in Baptism?

A. Natural water.

Q. What is the form?

A. *I baptise thee in the name of the Father, and of the Son, and of the Holy Ghost.*

Q. What is the visible sign?

A. Pouring water on the head.

Q. What is the Scriptural proof?

A. *Going therefore, teach ye all nations, baptising them in the name of the Father, and of the Son, and of the Holy Ghost.* (*Matt. xxviii. 19*)

Q. How many ways may a person be baptised?

A. Three – by water, by martyrdom, or by desire.

Q. What does the sacrament of Confirmation give?

A. The Holy Ghost, with the abundance of His graces.

Q. Does the Holy Ghost, then, come to dwell in us?

A. Yes; He comes in person.

Q. When was the Holy Ghost first given to us?

A. In Baptism.

Q. What is the matter in Confirmation?

A. Chrism.

Q. What is Chrism?

A. Oil of olives, mixed with balm, and blessed by the bishop
on Holy Thursday.

Q. What is the form in Confirmation?

A. *I sign thee with the sign of the cross, and I confirm thee with
the chrism of salvation, in the name of the Father, and of the
Son, and of the Holy Ghost.*

Q. What is the visible sign?

A. The imposition of hands and prayer.

Q. What is the Scriptural proof?

A. When St Philip, the deacon, had converted the city of
Samaria to the faith, the apostles, who were in Jerusalem, sent two bishops, St Peter and St John, to confirm
them. (*Acts viii. 14, 15*)

THE SEVEN GIFTS
OF THE
HOLY GHOST

Wisdom is a gift which teaches us to value rightly the things of this life, and fix our affections on God, and what belongs to Him.

Understanding makes us penetrate the truths of religion.

Counsel makes known to us the way of salvation and the enemies we have to contend with.

Fortitude enables us to overcome every obstacle that may oppose our spiritual progress.

Knowledge makes us acquainted with our duties towards God.

Piety enables us to discharge our duties towards God.

The Fear of the Lord impresses on our souls a great respect for the awful majesty of God, and a salutary dread of offending Him.

Q. What is the matter of the Blessed Eucharist?
A. Wheaten bread, and wine of the grape.

Q. What is the form?
A. *This is My Body, this is My Blood.*

Q. What is the visible sign?

A. The appearances of bread and wine.

Q. What is the Scriptural proof?

A. *This is My Body; this is My Blood.* (*Matt. xxvi. 26, 28*)

Q. Are the appearances called by other names?

A., Yes, the species, or accidents.

Q. Are these changed at the Consecration?

A. No.

Q. What is changed?

A. The substance of bread is changed into the Body and Blood of Christ.

Q. What is the change called?

A. Transubstantiation, which means the changing of one substance into another.

Q. How do we know that priests have the power to change bread and wine into the Body and Blood of Christ?

A. By the words which Christ addressed to His apostles at His last supper: – *Do this for a commemoration of me.* In telling them to *do this* He meant to do as He had just done, that is, to consecrate.

Q. Under what form do the laity receive?

A. Under the form of bread.

Q. Who receives under both forms?

A. Priests, and only when they celebrate Mass.

Q. Which of the Three Divine Persons do you receive in the Blessed Eucharist?

A. God the Son.

Q. Are the Father and the Holy Ghost with God the Son in the Blessed Eucharist?

A. They are, the Three being only One and the same God, there cannot be one without the other.

Q. Where is God the Son as man?

A. In Heaven and the Blessed Eucharist.

Q. Where is He as God?

A. In all places.

Q. Do those who communicate in the state of mortal sin receive the Body and Blood of Jesus Christ?

A. They do, but not His graces: they eat and drink judgement to themselves.

Q. What are the effects of receiving worthily?

A. An increase of grace, the soul is nourished in spiritual life, and the passions are weakened.

Q. What is the Holy Communion given to dying persons called?

A. Viaticum – that is, bread for a journey.

Q. Is the Blessed Eucharist anything else besides a sacrament?

A. Yes, it is a sacrifice when offered in the Mass.

Q. How many sacrifices have we?

A. One – the Mass.

Q. What worship is due to God?

A. Supreme worship – that is, a worship that has no equal.

Q. Wherein do we render to God the supreme worship that is due to Him?

A. In the Mass.

Q. Is the sacrifice offered to the angels or saints?

A. No, only to God.

Q. How many parts in the sacrament of Penance?

A. Four: Contrition, Confession, Satisfaction, and Absolution. Contrition is sorrow for sin. Confession is an open declaration of all our sins to a priest, in order to obtain absolution. Satisfaction is a faithful performance of the penance enjoined by the confessor. Absolution is the sentence of pardon pronounced by the priest.

Q. How many kinds of Contrition are there?

A. Two: Perfect Contrition and Imperfect Contrition; sometimes called Attrition.

Q. What is Perfect Contrition?

A. Sorrow for sin because sin is offensive to God, who is infinitely good in Himself.

Q. What is Imperfect Contrition or Attrition?

A. Sorrow for sin arising from some less perfect motives than the motive of perfect contrition, such as the fear of Hell, the loss of Heaven, our ingratitude in offending God.

Q. Will Imperfect Contrition or Attrition reconcile us to God without Confession?

A. No; but it will reconcile us to God in Confession, for it is sufficient as part of the Sacrament of Penance.

Q. Must Imperfect Contrition be a hearty sorrow?

A. It must; there can be no true sorrow or contrition of any kind that does not come from the heart.

Q. What is the matter of the sacrament of Penance?

A. Contrition, Confession, and Satisfaction.

Q. What is the form?

A. *I absolve thee from thy sins in the name of the Father, and of the Son, and of the Holy Ghost.*

Q. What is the sensible sign?

A. The absolution of the priest.

Q. What is the Scriptural proof?

A. When Christ said to His apostles on the day of His resurrection: *Receive ye the Holy Ghost, whose sins you shall forgive, they are forgiven; whose sins you shall retain, they are retained.* (John xx. 22, 23)

Q. When do priests forgive sin?

A. When they give absolution.

Q. When do they retain sin?

A. When they refuse absolution.

Q. What are the effects of the sacrament of Penance?

A. It remits sin, restores us to grace, and reconciles us to God.

Q. When must we go to confession?

A. As often as we fall into mortal sin, and, by command of the Church, at the very least once a year.

Q. What are the qualities of a good confession?

A. It must be entire, humble, sincere, and short. Entire – consisting of all our mortal sins. Humble – with confusion for having committed sin. Sincere – confessing our sins just as they are, without adding to or taking from them. Short – as brief as possible, consistent with clearness.

Q. What is the matter of Extreme Unction?

A. Oil blessed by a bishop.

Q. What is the form?

A. *By this holy anointing, and His own most pious mercy, may the Lord pardon thee whatsoever thou hast sinned by seeing, &c.*

[These words are repeated on anointing each sense.]

The five senses are seeing, hearing, smell, taste and touch.

Q. What is the sensible sign?

A. Anointing the five senses.

Q. What is the Scriptural proof?

A. St James says: *Is any man sick among you? Let him bring in the priests of the Church, and let them pray over him, anointing him with oil in the name of the Lord; and the prayer of faith shall save the sick man, and the Lord shall raise him up; and if he be in sins, they shall be forgiven him.* (*Chap. v. 14, 15*)

Q. What is the matter in Holy Orders?

A. The imposition of hands, and the delivery of the instruments.

Q. What is the form?

A. The accompanying words.

Q. What is the sensible sign?

A. The imposition of hands, with the delivery of the instruments of the particular power communicated, and prayer.

Q. What is the Scriptural proof?

A. *All power is given to me in Heaven and on earth; as the Father hath sent me, I also send you.* (*Matt. xxviii. 18; John xx. 21*)

Q. What is the matter in matrimony?

A. The mutual consent of the parties, expressed by words or signs.

Q. What is the form?

A. The mutual acceptation.

Q. What is the sensible sign?
A. The mutual consent of the parties, expressed by words or signs.

Q. What is the Scriptural proof?
A. *Therefore now they are not two, but one flesh. What therefore God hath joined together, let no man put asunder.* (Matt. xix. 6)

Q. How many kinds of punishment are due to mortal sin?
A. Two: eternal and temporal.

Q. What is the eternal punishment due to mortal sin?
A. Hell.

Q. What do you mean by temporal punishment?
A. Punishment which lasts only for a time.

Q. When is the eternal punishment remitted?
A. When the sin itself is forgiven.

Q. Is the temporal punishment forgiven at the same time?
A. Sometimes it is, but very often it is not.

Q. How, then, may we get remission of the temporal punishment which is not forgiven at the same time as the sin and eternal punishment are forgiven?
A. By any supernatural good works, such as faithful performance of the penance enjoined in Confession, acts of voluntary mortification, patient endurance of the sufferings of this life, and by indulgences.

Q. What is to be said of those who do not get remission of this temporal punishment during life?

A. They are said to *die indebted to God's justice on account of mortal sin*, and must suffer in Purgatory.

Q. What is an indulgence?

A. A remission of the whole, or part of the temporal punishment due to the divine justice for sin, after sin and the eternal punishment have been remitted.

Q. How many kinds of indulgences?

A. Two: Plenary and Partial; a Plenary Indulgence remits all the temporal punishments due to sin; a Partial Indulgence remits only a part of the temporal punishment.

Q. What is meant by an Indulgence of say seven years or a hundred days?

A. It means a remission of as much temporal punishment as would be remitted by undergoing the ancient Canonical penances for that number of years or days.

Qualities of Contrition

It must be Interior, Supernatural, Sovereign, and Universal.

Interior – coming from the heart.

Supernatural – inspired by the Holy Ghost.

Sovereign – the greatest of all sorrows.

Universal – extending to all mortal sins.

The Eight Beatitudes *(St Matt. chap. v)*

1. Blessed are the poor in spirit, for theirs is the kingdom of Heaven.
2. Blessed are the meek, for they shall possess the land.
3. Blessed are they that mourn, for they shall be comforted.
4. Blessed are they that hunger and thirst after justice, for they shall have their fill.
5. Blessed are the merciful, for they shall obtain mercy.
6. Blessed are the clean of heart, for they shall see God.
7. Blessed are the peacemakers, for they shall be called the children of God.
8. Blessed are they that suffer persecution for justice's sake, for theirs is the kingdom of Heaven.

The Spiritual Works of Mercy

1. To give counsel to the doubtful.
2. To instruct the ignorant.
3. To admonish sinners.
4. To comfort the afflicted.
5. To forgive offences.
6. To bear patiently the troublesome.
7. To pray for the living and the dead.

The Corporal Works of Mercy

1. To feed the hungry.
2. To give drink to the thirsty.
3. To clothe the naked.
4. To harbour the harbourless.
5. To visit the sick.
6. To visit the imprisoned.
7. To bury the dead.

Prayer for the Faithful Departed

Out of the depths I have cried toThee, O Lord; Lord, hear my voice.

Let Thy ears be attentive to the voice of my supplication.

If Thou, O Lord, wilt mark iniquities; Lord, who shall stand it.

For with Thee there is merciful forgiveness; and by reason of Thy law, I have waited for Thee, O Lord.

My soul hath relied on His word, my soul hath hoped in the Lord.

From the morning watch even until night, let Israel hope in the Lord.

Because with the Lord there is mercy; and with Him plentiful redemption.

And He shall redeem Israel from all his iniquities.

V. Give them, O Lord, eternal rest.

R. And let Thy light shine upon them forever.

Let us Pray.

O God, the Creator and Redeemer of all the faithful, give to the souls of Thy servants departed the remission of all their sins; that by pious supplications they may obtain the pardon they ever wished for; who livest and reignest, world without end.

R. Amen.

THE CHRISTIAN'S DAILY EXERCISE

Q. What is the first thing you should do in the morning?
A. I should make the sign of the cross, and offer my heart and soul to God.

Q. What should you do next?
A. I should rise diligently, dress myself modestly and entertain myself with good thoughts.

Q. What are those good thoughts?
A. Such as thoughts on the goodness of God who grants me this day to labour in it for the salvation of my soul; which day perhaps shall be my last.

Q. And what should you do after you have put on your clothes?
A. I should kneel down to my prayers, and perform my morning exercise.

Q. How should you perform the first part of your morning exercise?
A. I should bow down my soul and body to adore my God, and offer myself to His divine service.

Q. How should you perform the second part of your morning exercise?

A. I should give Him thanks for His infinite goodness to me and to all His creatures; and desire to join with all the angels and saints in blessing and praising Him.

Q. How should you perform the third part of your morning exercise?

A. I should crave pardon, from my heart, for all my sins; and beg that I may rather die than offend my God any more.

Q. How should you perform the fourth part of your morning exercise?

A. I should offer up to God all my thoughts, words, and actions of the day; and beg His blessing on them.

Q. And what prayers should you say after this?

A. I should say the Our Father, the Hail Mary, and the Apostles' Creed; and make Acts of Faith, Hope, and the Love of God.

Q. Should you do anything else?

A. I should pray for my friends and for my enemies, for the living and for the dead, and beg mercy, grace, and salvation for all. Then I should conclude by desiring our Blessed Lady to be a mother to me, and by recommending myself to my good angel, and to all the court of Heaven.

Q. Is this all a good Christian should do by way of morning exercise?

A. No; for he should also, if he has time and opportunity, meditate in the morning on his last end, or some other devout subject, and hear Mass with attention and devotion.

Q. What should you do at the beginning of every work or employment?

A. I should offer it up to God's service, and think that I will do it because it is His will, and in order to please Him.

Q. And what should you do as to your eating, drinking, sleeping, and diversion?

A. All these things I should use with moderation, and do them, because such is the will of God, and with a good intention to please Him.

Q. By what other means should you sanctify your ordinary actions and employments of the day?

A. By often raising up my heart to God whilst I am about them, and saying some short prayer to Him.

Q. What should you do as often as you hear the clock strike?

A. I should turn myself to God, and say to Him; *O my God, teach me to love Thee in time and eternity.*

Q. What should you do as often as you receive any blessing from God?

A. I should endeavour immediately to make Him a return of thanksgiving and love.

Q. What should you do when you find yourself tempted to sin?

A. I should make the sign of the cross upon my heart, and call upon God as earnestly as I can, saying, *Lord, save me, or I perish.*

Q. And what if you have fallen into sin?

A. I should cast myself in spirit at the feet of Christ, and humbly beg His pardon, saying, *Lord, be merciful to me, a sinner.*

Q. What should you say when God sends you any cross, or suffering, or sickness, or pain?

A. I should say, *Lord, Thy will be done; I take this for my sins.*

Q. And what other little prayers should you say to yourself from time to time in the day?

A. *Lord, what wilt Thou have me to do? Oh, teach me to do Thy holy will in all things. Lord, keep me from sin. May the name of the Lord be forever blessed. Come, my dear Jesus, and take full possession of my soul. Glory be to the Father and to the Son, and to the Holy Ghost. As it was in the beginning, is now, and ever shall be, world without end. Amen.*

Q. How should you perform your evening exercise?

A. I should say the Our Father, the Hail Mary, and the Apostles' Creed, together with the Acts of Faith, Hope, and the Love of God, &c., as I did in the morning.

Q. And should you not also join with the family in saying the Litany, and other evening prayers, which are usually said in Catholic families?

A. Yes; as also in the daily examination of conscience.

Q. How should you prepare for your evening examination of conscience?

A. I should place myself in the presence of God, as I usually do at the beginning of all my prayers, and beg His light and help to know my sins, and to be sorry for them.

Q. How should you make your examination of conscience?

A. I should consider how I have spent the day from morning till night; in what manner I have performed my prayers and all other duties; what blessings I have received from God; and what offences I have been guilty of against Him by commission or omission.

Q. What acts should you perform after your examination of conscience?

A. I should give thanks to God for all His blessings, and beg pardon for all my sins, endeavouring to make a hearty act of contrition for them.

Q. How should you conclude the evening exercise?

A. I should recommend my soul into the hands of God, with the best disposition I can of love and conformity to His blessed will, as if I were to die that night.

Q. How should you finish the day?

A. I should observe great modesty in going to bed, entertain myself with the thoughts of death; and, endeavour to compose myself to rest at the foot of the cross, and to give my last thoughts to my crucified Saviour.

SPIRITUAL AND THOUGHT-PROVOKING QUOTATIONS

DES MACHALE

In the crazy, rushed world of today this wonderful collection of quotations from the greatest philosophers, poets and thinkers provides an opportunity to stop and reflect.

Do you know who said:

To a man with an empty stomach, food is God.

I try, I fail. I try again. I fail better.

Alcoholism isn't a spectator sport. Sooner or later, the whole family gets to play.

Man is born broken. He lives by mending. The grace of God is glue.

No snowflake in the avalanche ever feels responsible.

Most children suffer from too much mother and too little father.

The best kind of sex education is a loving family

Nothing lasts forever – not even your troubles.

SOMETHING UNDERSTOOD
A SPIRITUAL ANTHOLOGY

EDITED BY SEÁN DUNNE

This anthology contains a rich selection of writing on many aspects of spirituality. They include God, pain, prayer, love, loss, joy and silence. Drawing on the great traditions of Christian spirituality, Seán Dunne has assembled pieces by dozens of writers, among them Thomas Merton, Simone Weil, Teresa of Avila, John Henry Newman, and Dietrich Bonhoeffer. He has also chosen from the work of creative writers such as Patrick Kavanagh, John McGahern, Kate O'Brien and George Herbert. With a wide selection of material that ranges from just a few lines to many pages, *Something Understood* is a perfect source for reflection on aspects of spirituality that have been a concern of men and women through the centuries.